Journey to Easter

A Book of Daily Meditations for Lent

BY

LAURENCE N. FIELD

AUGSBURG PUBLISHING HOUSE
Minneapolis, Minnesota

COPYRIGHT ACKNOWLEDGMENTS

To the Division of Christian Education, National Council of Churches for quotations from the Revised Standard Version of the Bible, copyright 1946 and 1952.

To Macmillan Company, for the poem "Mastery" by Sara Teasdale.

To Ada Jackson for her poem "Again the Story Is Told"

To Ruth Pitter for her poem "If a Man Dies Shall He Live Again"

To Harper and Brothers for the poem "The Captains of the Years" by Arthur R. Macdougall

To Ann Watkins for the poem "The Choice of the Cross" by Dorothy L. Sayers

To Rex Boundy for his poem "A Virile Christ"

To John Day Company for the poem "The Starry Night" by Herman Hagedorn

To John R. Slater for the poem "A Ballad of Wonder" by Eleanor Slater

To
Johan Carl Keyser Preus

A cherished friend

A consecrated pastor

A notable educator

And a great leader

Foreword

LENTEN sermons and books have a strong tendency to be heavy, negative, and highly charged with emotional tension. And no wonder, for they contemplate the supreme tragedy of the ages and Him who is its Center. Truly, no one can follow that terrible drama and not weep! But there is another aspect of it that is too little stressed. The Via Dolorosa is also a Glory Road, a march of triumph; for Lent does not end at the grave on Good Friday, but with the resurrection. We have embodied this thought in our title: "Journey to Easter," as well as in the book's content.

These little homilies follow chronologically the history of the Passion, but only approximately. For the many events, concentrated as they are pretty much into the last night and day of our Lord's suffering, are not easy to spread out over forty-six days and keep the proper order intact. And the six Sundays of Lent, with their texts, are anything but amenable to chronological regimentation. Nor is the exact sequence of events completely agreed on by scholars. But surely this does not matter a great deal, since the Bible has left it so. We make therefore no apologies for an occasional aberration, and only ask the reader's indulgence. We have spread plot and chronology over a period of forty-six days, in presenting the divine Epic that transcends them both! We have striven to make these sermonettes brief, simple, and personal. We hope that this will make them more graphic and helpful.

We offer this little nosegay of Devotions with the prayer that the gracious Redeemer will bless them upon the hearts and souls of all who read, and draw them closer to Him.

Soli Deo gloria!

LAURENCE N. FIELD
Luther Theological Seminary
St. Paul, Minnesota

Contents

Lent

LENT means "spring," and its use in the Church goes back to the fourth century. There is beautiful symbolism in this, because Lent leads to Easter, which is the Spring of the Soul. As spring brings back life after the icy sleep of winter, so our Lord by His resurrection brings back life to the souls of mankind dead in sin, but alive again through His victory over death. It is as the ancient Greek hymn writer, John of Damascus (8th century), sings:

> 'Tis the spring of souls today,
> Christ hath burst His prison,
> And from three days' sleep in death
> As a sun hath risen;
> All the winter of our sins,
> Long and dark, is flying
> From His light, to whom we give
> Laud and praise undying.

The Church has retained this symbolism in keeping the word "Lent." Thus let us, too, begin this season with a vision of Easter.

1

The Lenten season consists of forty "week days," plus six "Lord's Days" (Sundays), just prior to Easter. The forty days match the forty days of prayer and fasting of our Lord in connection with His temptation (Matthew 4). For this reason many Churches observe the custom of fasting during Lent, or at least "giving up something"—for instance refraining from certain foods and pleasures. Most of us will have to confess that we give up very little for Him at any time; and perhaps many of those who do, do so as a perfunctory thing, or even with mistaken ideas as to the value and religious significance of what they do. On the basis of Mark 2:18-20, Matthew 6:16-18, and other passages, it seems to this writer that this kind of devotion is not the significant part of Lent. Robert Herrick (1591-1674) expresses it very well:

TO KEEP A TRUE LENT

Is this a fast, to keep
The larder lean
And clean
From fat of veal and sheep?

Is it to quit the dish
Of flesh, yet still
To fill
The platter high with fish?

Is it to fast an hour,
Or ragged go,
Or show
A downcast look, and sour?

No! 'Tis a fast to dole
Thy sheaf of wheat
And meat
Unto the hungry soul!

It is to fast from strife,
From old debate
And hate;
To circumcise thy life!

To show a heart grief-rent,
To starve thy sin,
Not bin;
And that's to keep thy Lent!

Lent begins with Ash Wednesday. It is so called from a medieval custom of daubing one's forehead with ashes from the palms of the previous year's Palm Sunday, burned and saved for this purpose. The symbolism was contrition and sorrow for the sins that crucified the Lord Jesus.

What then shall be the measure of *our* devotion as we journey through Lent? Let it also for us be sorrow for sin, and adoration of Him who bought us with His blood and conquered death and the Evil One to win for us life and salvation here and forever.

PRAYER

Lord, give us humble, holy contrition, as we follow Thee through Lent. Give us grace to follow with devotion Thy steady steps and serenity, to the strengthening of our souls, our vision, and our faith. Amen.

The shadow of the cross

This child is set for the fall and rising of many in Israel, and for a sign that is spoken against (and a sword will pierce through your own soul also), that thoughts out of many hearts may be revealed. Simeon's prophecy, Luke 2:34

THE shadow of the cross had hung over Jesus' path ever since that babyhood scene in the temple when old man Simeon had mixed bitterness with blessing in his pronouncement to Mary. Now the time was come to enter that shadow and make it His own. There are two aspects to shadows. One is forbidding and foreboding. The other is the opposite—it is shade rather than shadow, cooling rather than cold, bringer of balm and blessing. Jesus' cross had the elements of both. Of the sinister side and the suffering, His is the supreme example. Of the glory side, it is also the supreme example. It is, as Elizabeth Clephane (1830-1869) sings:

4

> The shadow of a mighty Rock
> Within a weary land;
> A home within the wilderness,
> A rest upon the way,
> From the burning of the noontide heat,
> And the burden of the day.

Another thing about shadows: they are convincing testimony that somewhere there is light. For to cast a shadow there *has* to be light, otherwise there is darkness only, and no shadow. This, too, distinguishes the cross of the Redeemer. That light is the atoning, forgiving, healing love of our heavenly Father.

The shadow and sign of the cross! How astonishing they are in their potency, how appealing in their simplicity, and how universally recognized! Two sticks laid one upon the other; two fingers crossed; two lines in the dust, traced by the naked toe of an ancient slave and interpreted and shared by his brother; a crusader's sword and its hilt, thrust upright into the ground and before which he kneels for his devotions; the bejeweled pendant about milady's neck; the signatures of the nobles who signed England's Magna Carta but who could not write, and so "made their mark," the cross; the emblem upon our altars, from wood to burnished gold; the almost five hundred forms and varieties of the cross created by the loving imagination of Christian artists and craftsmen; the cruciform of our church buildings; a telegraph pole silhouetted against the sky; the neon monstrosity that blinks at us from twen-

5

tieth century belfries and steeples; the bosses and caps of the headstones in our cemeteries—all, all bear copious witness to the universality and significance of the cross and the beneficence and blessing cast by its shadow in every age and clime. "I seal thee with the sign of the holy cross, as a token that thou shalt believe on the crucified Lord Jesus Christ," said our pastor when we began our baptized life in Him.

The shadow, the lengthening shadow, of the cross! What divinity of grandeur, what hope and assurance, attach themselves to this ancient symbol. For it tells us of Christ and all He has done and continues to do.

PRAYER

Jesus, may our hearts be burning with more fervent love for Thee! May our eyes be ever turning to Thy cross of agony! Till in glory, parted never from the blessed Saviour's side, graven in our hearts forever, dwell the cross, the Crucified! Amen.

From a hymn-prayer by GIROLAMO SAVONAROLA who died a martyr to the Gospel in 1498

Wondrous love

How can I give you up, O Ephraim! How can I hand you over, O Israel! . . . My heart recoils within me, my compassion grows warm and tender. . . . I will not again destroy Ephraim; for I am God and not man, the Holy One in your midst, and I will not come to destroy. . . . I will heal their faithlessness; I will love them freely, for my anger has turned from them." Hosea 11:8-9; 14:4

I HAVE been reading the Book of Hosea in the Old Testament. It is the agonizing story of frustrated love that would not give up! God commanded His prophet to marry a prostitute, *and to keep on loving her* even though she was brazenly unfaithful to him. The symbolism is this: Israel was that woman, God was that husband. And all of it is the foreshadow of the Messiah, who loves the whole world—even the worst sinner—just like that. So then He loves me and He loves you, my reader! No other

7

religion has that kind of gospel; and no earthly philosopher. It is undreamable, it does not make sense, it is past the understanding of man. It is too good to be true, it is impossible! The Spirit of God is necessary even to believe and accept it. But the persevering love of the divine Christ transcends the impossible.

Following the footsteps of the Passion story, glancing down the pages of history ever since, looking round about us in our own day, and examining our own hearts, we stand in awe as we face the love of Christ and contemplate this that almighty God should bother with humankind. Beautifully and simply this is expressed in music by Paul Christiansen in his setting of a southern folk song and its text:

> What wondrous love is this, O my soul, O my soul,
> That caused the Lord of life to bear the heavy cross,
> What wondrous love is this, O my soul!
> That Christ should lay aside His crown for my soul!
> What wondrous love, what wondrous love, O my soul!

What a contrast to this is the unregenerate world and its presentation of love! What an abused, prostituted, and insulting image is set up for us in many a book and magazine and screen and TV and best seller! What cheap, pornographic imitations leer and gibber before us in the private lives of not a few of our nation's entertainers, amusement celebrities, and public figures! No wonder twentieth century teen-agers are mixed up and bewildered in the constant atmosphere of passion and sin that passes for love all around them, and can not distinguish wrong from right!

But even our best love, between friend and friend, husband and wife, parent and child—though they be cemented and hallowed by matured years of joy and adversity, trial and triumph, sacrifice and sharing together—even our very best love stands amazed at the immensity of His, and only dares ask that in some measure it may be like His.

Who can read the story of His love and sacrifice, who can face the radiance of His Gospel, and not be gripped by it, and ask permission to love Him in return and dedicate one's self to His service?

PRAYER

O Thou good Omnipotent, who carest for every one of us as if Thou carest for him alone; and so for all of us as if all were but one! I behold how some things pass away that others may replace them, but Thou dost never depart. O God my Father, supremely good, Beauty of all things beautiful: to thee will I entrust all that I have received from Thee; and so shall I lose nothing. Thou madest me for Thyself, and my heart is restless until it find repose in Thee. Amen.

ST. AUGUSTINE

That which we have seen

That which was from the beginning, which we have heard, which we have seen with our eyes, which we have looked upon and touched with our hands, concerning the word of life —the life . . . made manifest to us . . . we proclaim also to you, so that you may have fellowship with us; and our fellowship is with the Father and with his Son Jesus Christ. And we are writing this that our joy may be complete.   I John 1:1-4

LONG, long after the event, thus wrote John, the beloved Apostle. How real and lively is his testimony! After two-thirds of a century the aged Apostle recalls, just as vividly and graphically as though it were yesterday, the experience that has meant so much to him. Tenderly, touchingly, he reminisces.

Many people forget so soon, even when they would like to remember. Alas, that our lives should be made up so much of brevities strung on a bead chain of years! Hello and goodby, hail and farewell, learn and forget, pause and go on—such is the tenor of our years. We are like

> Ships that pass in the night
> And speak to each other in passing;
> Only a signal shown
> And a distant voice in the darkness.
> So on the ocean of life
> We pass and speak one to another;
> Only a look and a voice,
> Then darkness again and a silence.
>
> H. W. LONGFELLOW
> from Theologian's Tale: "Elizabeth"

John's experience with Christ could conceivably have been that too, for he himself tells of others who journeyed with the Lord a while only, and then left (John 6:66). But his was no casual acquaintance—he really met his Master face to face. And he was transformed, nothing was the same thereafter.

So it must also be with us, if we are to get out of our faith and religion, and out of our fellowship with Christ, what He meant that we should have. Religion is no good when it is piecemeal or perfunctory. There must be a deep, dynamic, personal commitment. Our Lord can not be just one among other interests. He must take over, and other things must be subordinate to Him, so that He may either bless them or root them out. So let our walk with Him through Lent also be real and personal and genuine, as was John's. Then our religion, our

11

Church, and our life's pilgrimage will indeed become a joyful thing.

Finally, the life which is in Christ is at its finest when it is shared. Indeed it can not be hoarded or hidden. And we need the contagion of fellowship. Two beautiful things characterized John's walk with his Lord: He was so close and real to him that it was as though he could reach out and touch Him; and, secondly, he was filled with a ceaseless ambition to share Him with others. "That which we have seen and heard we proclaim also to you," he wrote, "so that you may have fellowship together with us with the Father and with His Son, Jesus Christ. And we are writing this that our joy may be complete!"

PRAYER

Lord, it belongs not to my care whether I die or live; to love and serve Thee is my share, and this Thy grace must give. Christ leads me through no darker rooms than He went through before; he that into God's Kingdom comes must enter by this door. Come, Lord, when grace hath made me meet Thy blessed face to see; for if Thy work on earth be sweet, what will Thy glory be?

RICHARD BAXTER (1615-1691)

Jesus is king

Rejoice greatly, O daughter of Zion!
Shout aloud, O daughter of Jerusalem!
Lo, your King comes to you;
Triumphant and victorious is he,
Humble and riding on an ass,
On a colt, the foal of an ass . . .
His dominion shall be from sea to sea,
And from the River to the ends of the earth.
Zechariah 9:9-10

JESUS' entry into Jerusalem on Palm Sunday was an important event in history, no matter from what point one looks at it, and even though its arch of triumph was a cross. To our Lord personally, also, it was an important event. It was fulfillment of Scripture. He had insisted against every argument and opposition on being there, and had planned and anticipated every detail of His participation in it. The immense size of the Passover crowd made the occasion international in scope, and that par-

13

ticular year He was the central figure. His bold and triumphant entry was a coup and demonstration of fearlessness over against His enemies. Long before He came, He knew that He had a date with death, but He did not slink in like an exhausted fugitive and give Himself up. He rode in like a king, albeit a humble and unusual one, for He *was* King, the Messiah-King of God! His reception was a religious one as it should be, and His acclaim spiritual. "Hosanna to the Son of David!" they cried, and spread garments and palm branches on the way. "Blessed is he that cometh in the name of the Lord!" For the moment and as far as it went, the homage was spontaneous and sincere, except, of course, for that outer fringe of the ignorant and hateful. In order to properly appraise Jesus' entry into Jerusalem and the events of Holy Week, it is not necessary therefore to merge and confuse that Palm Sunday crowd with the dregs of that crowd that stayed up all night to bait and crucify the Christ on Good Friday morning.

But it was not an occasion of earthly pomp and glory. Jesus wept as He rode. For He knew the fickleness of man, He saw what lurked behind the tinsel and the bunting, and He heard the mutterings that mingled with the shouting. And ahead lay Golgotha! Through it all He was true to Himself, true to His heavenly Father. In all aspects He continued to maintain His role as the Messiah King and at the same time the Suffering Servant—divine in His humility, humble in His divinity. Nevertheless he was *King!* And though His scepter was a cross and His Kingdom had no concern with geography, His has been the most real and lasting kingship of them all. The world and its Greats must still step aside and bow and yield the right-of-way to Him as He rides on ahead and with His followers outlives them one by one forever. Every dictator and fulminator and man on horseback in history is witness to the fact.

Happy are we who can say that Jesus the Christ, is *our* King, even as He is our Savior. Let us love Him frankly, follow Him boldly, proclaim Him with confidence, and worship Him with prayer, praise, and thanksgiving.

I watched the Captains
A-riding, riding
Down the years;
The men of mystic grip
Of soul, a-riding
Between a hedge of spears.

I saw their banners
A-floating, floating
Over all,
Till each of them had passed
And Christ came, riding
A donkey lean and small.

I watched the Captains
A-turning, staring,
Proud and set,
At Christ a-riding there—
So calmly riding
The Road men can't forget!

15

I watched the Captains
Dismounting, waiting—
None now led—
The Captains bowing low!
The Caesars waiting!
—While Christ rode on ahead.

A. R. MACDOUGALL, JR. (1880–)

PRAYER

*O Savior, precious Savior, whom yet unseen we love; O Name
of might and favor, all other names above! We worship Thee,
we bless Thee, to Thee, O Christ we sing; we praise Thee
and confess Thee, our holy Lord and King. Amen.*

FRANCES R. HAVERGAL (1836-1879)

On to Jerusalem

*When the days drew near for him to be received up, he set
his face to go to Jerusalem.* Luke 9:51

Hard it is, very hard,
To travel up the slow and stony road
To Calvary, to redeem mankind; far better
To make but one resplendent miracle,
Lean through the cloud, lift the right hand of power
And with a sudden lightning smite the world perfect!
Yet this was not God's way, who had the power,
But set it by, choosing the cross, the thorn,
The sorrowful wounds. Something there is, perhaps,
That power destroys in passing, something supreme,
To whose great value in the eyes of God
That cross, that thorn, and those five wounds bear witness.

From "The Devil to Pay" by
DOROTHY L. SAYERS (1893)

HOW serenely He takes that final trip, pausing
here to caress a child, there to pick a wild
flower and point out its lesson, yonder to heal some
foul disease, anon to comfort the unhappy, and to
speak quiet words to His followers! Does he not

17

realize what lies ahead—insult, betrayal, wounds, and death? Yes, who could know it better than He —for His whole life has focused on that last journey! It is that divine *must,* that mysterious determination, that love which will not let go, that draws Him on.

What giant strides He takes! Even now in our so-called enlightened age, after two thousand years of the lengthening shadow of His presence, the world is able only to toddle after Him in its best thinking, trying in vain to catch up with His vision, and seemingly unable to assimiliate or act on His simplest precept, on anything like a world-wide scale. And yet the world knows that if He were really followed by common consent even for one brief Lent, such wonders of peace and felicity would take place for this planet that no historian could adequately record or describe it.

During Lent it is customary to set aside a certain modicum of time to contemplate Him, particularly on the last lap of His journey. "Come," we say, "let us take a little time off to feel sorry for Him now before Easter, as He staggers up Golgotha hill! 'Can ye not watch with me one brief hour'" we quote, "say from seven forty-five to a quarter of nine of a Wednesday evening." One brief hour, when a whole life of contrition would not suffice! One brief hour, when the world is burning, and groups and nations are busy crucifying Him anew on a scale that the centurion at the cross, and his little corporal's guard—nor all history, for that matter—never dreamed of!

18

Feel sorry for Thee? Merciful Savior, do Thou feel sorry for *us*—this mad planet that after two world wars in one generation, and a taste of atomic destruction besides, has not yet had its belly full but can still find leadership and depravity enough for one more try! This bedeviled world, in which even our own beloved America can return from the holocaust and re-dedicate itself seven times worse than ever to soaring crime waves, greed, cynicism, and lechery! What tame little models our forefathers had in trying to figure out Armageddon and the antichrist compared to us!

PRAYER

Christ, have mercy on us! Use Thy almighty power to halt the avalanche of evil which, under demon-possessed leaders, would still destroy us all! Stretch forth Thy nail-pierced hands to embrace this dung-heap world, lest having thrown itself into one abyss in this life it be confronted with still another in the life to come! Show us in our day, too, how to set our face steadfastly to go to Jerusalem, to render sacrifices of love and right living, and help the world again to learn what it is to be decent, and to recognize the presence of God and the value of the soul! After the long shadow of war and atheism and brutality, in mercy show the world what the sun is like again—and faith and mutual trust and brotherly love—Thou who art the all-conquering Christ and Lord forever! Amen.

Previews of the cross

From that time Jesus began to show his disciples that he must go to Jerusalem and suffer many things from the elders and chief priests and scribes, and be killed, and on the third day be raised. Matthew 16:21

AS HAS been referred to, Jesus was supremely aware that His way led past Golgotha. He began early to prepare the minds of His disciples for this and for the need of a cross in their own discipleship. Their first reaction was one of open resistance and revulsion. Peter, for instance (Matthew 16), could not endure the thought of his Lord being mistreated and killed. Brusquely "he took him and began to rebuke him, saying, 'God forbid, Lord! This shall never happen to you!'" The outburst was well meant, but presumptuous, and Peter had to be put in his place. As brusquely as he had spoken, the Lord replied: "Get behind me, Satan!

20

You are a hindrance to me; for you are not on the side of God, but of men!" Thereafter an air of mysterious dread hung over the whole subject, and they avoided it. As Mark states, "They understood not the saying, and were afraid to ask him" (Mark 9:32).

A little farther on in Matthew's Gospel Jesus spoke of it again, after the Glory Scene on the Mount of Transfiguration (Matthew 17). But again they did not realize, and were only saddened and worried. "And they were greatly distressed," the Gospels tell us. The significance of the words concerning His resurrection escaped them completely.

When they drew near to Jerusalem the last time He again "took the twelve disciples aside" (Matthew 20), "and on the way He said to them: 'Behold, we are going up to Jerusalem; and the Son of Man will be delivered to the chief priests and scribes; and they will condemn Him to death and deliver Him to the Gentiles to be mocked and scourged and crucified, and He will be raised on the third day.'" This time Matthew and Mark record a curious incident that took place in connection with the announcement—James and John and their mother came and asked for special consideration when He came into His Kingdom, namely to sit one at the right hand and one at His left hand in His glory. Their request was promptly denied, and they were reminded of the cross which would be for them, too, who were disciples. And the other disciples became indignant at the two brothers because of their presumption. Not until after the resurrection was there anything like a realization among the disciples of the significance of the cross, and not until Pentecost was it complete.

We too must plead guilty to the same slowness of heart as they. For we also find ourselves wanting to be religious the easy way, to follow the line of least resistance, and to take as little trouble as possible. It is not a welcome invitation to take up our cross, to make a break with the world, and to be content with anonymity in following Him! We would like to see that at least some glamour might be added. But Jesus says: "If any man would follow after me, let him deny himself and take up his cross and follow me. For whosoever would save his life shall lose it, and whoever loses his life for my sake will find it."

PRAYER

Dear Lord, we who find it so hard to see that any good can come out of suffering, that the finest blessing is in sacrifice, and that to give is better than to receive—give us a better vision, we pray Thee! And we whose crosses are but small indeed, pray that Thou wilt particularly bless those whose crosses are heavy compared to ours. Give us grace and means to help those round about us who struggle with the burdens and distresses of life! To Thee we pray, who gavest up all and wast nailed to the cross for our sakes. Amen.

Cleansing of the temple

*And Jesus entered the temple of God and drove out all who
sold and bought in the temple, and he overturned the tables
of the money changers and the seats of those who sold
pigeons. He said to them, "It is written, 'My house shall be
called a house of prayer'; but you make it a den of robbers."*
Matthew 21:12-13

WHEN Christ entered Jerusalem He went
directly to the temple. He saw much that
both saddened and angered Him. The Old Testament system of sacrifices and the huge scale on
which they now had to be conducted, together
with the greed of man and the secularization of the
Church, had led to strange and terrible abuses. The
noise and smell of sacrificial animals, the exchang-
ing of money, and the milling about of great crowds,
made it a hive of confusion and a poor background
for the edification of the soul. Obviously the ancient
sacrificial system was outmoded and should be done

23

away with. This was what Jesus came to do, as the Lamb of God and the last great Sacrifice. But what angered Him was the way sin and corruption had taken over. The scene was like a county fair or a huge market-place, with haggling, cheating, and noise on all sides. He was already familiar with it, having seen it many times over, and had already done something about it too, according to John (chapter 2). There was need to act again.

The next morning He and His disciples returned. Then He seized a whip and drove out all those that bought and sold, kicking over the tables and seats of the money-changers, and cried out in the words of Isaiah (56:7): "It is written: 'My house shall be called a house of prayer,' but you make it a den of robbers!" He now proceeded to demonstrate what the House of God should be like, and spent that day and the next preaching and teaching. "And the blind and lame came to him in the temple, and he healed them," the Gospels add. The temple racketeers were of course busily at it again as soon as they dared. What they could not know was that their whole sacrificial set-up was doomed from that day, and was on the way out. The last great Sacrifice was on hand and would presently be offered.

There is a little temple in the hearts of all of us. What a tragedy that it can become so cluttered up with worldliness, sin, and misguided endeavors, that it too can cause but sadness and sorrow to the Savior! Is not this, then, a good place to pause, O my soul, and pray Him to enter and cleanse and

24

re-dedicate? Not in anger, Lord, lest I perish! But in love and mercy!

And are there not also churches and houses of religion in our communities that need to pause and consider that not everything that is done there is unto edification—that money and externals and glamour and bigness are not the essence of church work and may even make it difficult for the Spirit to operate?

Give us a virile Christ for these rough days!
You painters, sculptors—show the warrior bold,
And you who turn mere words to gleaming gold! . . .
We need a Man of Strength with us, to hold
The very breach of death without amaze.
Did He not scourge from temple courts the thieves?
And make the arch-fiend's self again to fall?
And blast the fig-tree that was only leaves?
And still the raging tumult of the sea?
Did He not bear the greatest pain of all,
Silent, upon the Cross on Calvary?

REX BOUNDY

PRAYER

Lord God, heavenly Father: We thank Thee that by Thy Holy Spirit Thou dost in all places gather Thy Christian Church, and upon the one chief cornerstone, even Jesus Christ, dost build unto Thyself a spiritual temple, wrought of living stones. We beseech Thy great mercy: graciously look upon Thy Church throughout our land, to build it up in the faith which is in Christ. . . . O Lord God, give Thy Word free course among us. . . . And when at last we are laid away in the grave, grant us a blessed resurrection at the last day, that we may dwell with Thee forever in the new Jerusalem, where there is no temple; for Thou, Lord, the almighty God, and the Lamb, are the temple thereof. Amen.

From the *Altar Book*
The prayer at the dedication of a church

The withering fig tree

And seeing . . . a fig tree in leaf, he went to see if he could find anything on it. When he came to it, he found nothing but leaves. . . . And he said to it, "May no one ever eat fruit from you again."   Mark 11:13, 14

IT WAS Monday morning of Holy Week, and they were on their way back to Jerusalem from Bethany where they had spent the night. A fig tree attracted their attention. It was already in full leaf, although it was early in the season. Jesus was hungry and went over to it, expecting to find figs. Instead He found only leaves. Addressing Himself to the tree, He said, "May no one eat fruit from you again!" The disciples were surprised, as they were not used to this kind of talk from their Master. But they said nothing, and all went on together.

The next morning they again made their way from Bethany to Jerusalem. As they passed the fig tree they noticed that it was already withered to its very roots. "Look, Master," Peter said, "the fig tree which you cursed has withered." Then Jesus explained the whole incident. It was not a display of peevishness, nor primarily an act of destruction. It was a lesson in the power of faith and prayer (Mark 11:20-25). "Have faith in God," He said. "Whatever you ask in prayer, believe that you will receive it, and you will." Then, as though to be sure that the incident would not be misunderstood, He added: "Whenever you stand praying, forgive, if you have anything against anyone; so that your Father also, who is in heaven, may forgive you your trespasses." Thus, the withering of the fig tree was a sort of parable in action.

There is neither morality nor immorality in the destruction of a tree, and preachers have wasted much time in feeling that they should defend Jesus in the matter. But it is impossible to follow this story and not be struck by the implication of what He *could* have done with His almighty power, if He had chosen to use it, for instance against His enemies. It is not insignificant to note that when the Savior set out to destroy, He chose—a tree!

This incident is a reminder of the parable of the unproductive fig tree in the thirteenth chapter of Luke. For three years in succession the owner came looking for fruit, but found none. Then he said, "Cut it down! Why should it use up the ground?" But the gardener pleaded, "Let it alone, Sir, this year also, till I dig about it and put on manure. And if it bears fruit, well and good; but if not, you can cut it down."

Are not we that fig tree much of the time? Alas, how often has not the heavenly Father come looking for fruit and found none! Then our Lord Christ speaks up and says, "Let it alone, Sir, this year also; and I will dig about this tree and put on manure— and then?" But the patience of our Lord can not go on forever.

There is another parable of unproductiveness also, in the story of the Sower (Mark 4). Here, too, we must confess that we are but fallow ground, and plead, "Lord, have mercy on us, and love us still!"

PRAYER

Sower divine! Sow good seed in me, seed for eternity. 'Tis a rough, barren soil; yet by Thy care and toil, make it a fruitful field, an hundredfold to yield. Sower divine: Plow up this heart of mine! . . . Sower divine: Quit not this wretched field, till Thou hast made it yield! Sow Thou by day and night, in darkness and in light; stay not Thy hand, but sow! Then shall the harvest grow. . . . Sower divine: Let not this barren clay lead Thee to turn away; let not my fruitlessness provoke Thee not to bless; let not this field be dry! Refresh it from on high! Sower divine: Water this heart of mine!

HORATIO BONAR (1808-1889): *"The Heavenly Sowing"*

Jesus' last public work-day

We must work the works of him who sent me, while it is
day; night comes, when no one can work.   John 9:4

TUESDAY of Passion Week is generally consid-
ered to have been the last work-day of Jesus'
public ministry. If so, it surpassed them all for long,
hard, heart-breaking busyness! He had no sooner
reached the temple that morning than His enemies
were around Him heckling and arguing. What authority did He have, they wanted to know, and
where were His credentials? But they would not
listen when He told them, and when He countered
with logic and truth, they could only answer with
sophistry and name calling. Pointed and sarcastic
were the parables He told that day, and acrid was
His sermonizing, in an effort to jolt them out of
their closed minds and stubborn complacency.

Such parables as: The two sons who were told by their father to go to work in the vineyard (Matthew 21:28); the wicked husbandmen who slew the messengers and were themselves slain (Matthew 21:33); the slighted wedding invitation and he who was thrown into outer darkness (Matthew 22:1); and doubtless other parables, too, were spoken that grim Tuesday. The scribes and Pharisees did not fail to get His meaning, but the warning and lessons were lost on them—they only became more angry and set. They continued to bait Him with loaded questions such as: Tribute to Caesar (Matthew 22:15), which was always a red rag to the Jews; Marriage and Divorce, and Is There a Heaven? (Matthew 22:23). Sharper and sharper became His retorts, until they climaxed in the thunder of "Woe unto you, scribes and Pharisees, hypocrites" in Matthew twenty-three.

But good things also came out of that tumultuous day. There was, for instance, the visit of the Greeks, who came from afar and contacted Philip—he of the Greek name—and said respectfully, "Sir, we wish to see Jesus." And there was His masterful answer to the question "What is the great Commandment of the Law?" His answer was "Love." And that touching scene over against the treasury, where they watched the humble widow put in her two mites, which added up to one penny, but received praise forever. Sadly Jesus closed with the heart-rending lament: "O Jerusalem, Jerusalem, killing the prophets and stoning those who are sent to you. How often would I have gathered your children together as a hen gathers her brood under her wings, and you would not! Behold, your house is forsaken and desolate."

When He took His leave, the disciples sat with Him on the hillside over against the city, while He told them again with quiet soberness of the destruction of the Temple and Jerusalem, and what awaited also them in their own ministry. Reminding them again of the fig tree and the orderly processes of God, who guideth all things, He gave them two watchwords: "Watch and pray," and "Be not troubled." Awe-struck, they listened, until the darkness came and the never-to-be-forgotten day was over.

We too, who have lived and will continue to live through perilous apocryphal times—we too must learn to watch and pray, and trust in almighty God to guide our times and us, until we emerge on the other side. For all history and all times and places are in His hands.

PRAYER

Lord God, who rulest over time and space, who dost mark the sparrow's fall, and layest out the pathway of comet and star—do not forget little me in Thy bigness, either, but watch over me at all times. Forgive my sins and my lack of faith, and strengthen me to know and do Thy will. Through Jesus Christ, my Lord. Amen.

Day of retirement

Then the chief priests and elders of the people gathered in the palace of the high priest, who was called Caiaphas, and took counsel together in order to arrest Jesus by stealth and kill him. Then one of the twelve, who was called Judas Iscariot, went to the chief priests and said, "What will you give me if I deliver him to you?" And they paid him thirty pieces of silver. And from that moment he sought an opportunity to betray him. Matthew 26:3f., 14ff.

WE HAVE come to Wednesday of Holy Week. It is not known what our Lord did on that day, as the Gospels have left it blank. Various names have been given it, such as "The Day of Withdrawal," "The Day of Silence," etc. Perhaps He retired for rest, for prayer, and for strength to meet the terrible ordeal that lay ahead. He could do no more for His enemies now, except to pray for them, and—to die for them! There was time for one more session with

His disciples. He yearned for this meeting, and planned it carefully.

Meanwhile His enemies were not idle. They called a secret meeting in the palace of Caiaphas to plot how to do away with this bold prophet. They did not dare lay hands on Him in open daylight, for Jesus had many friends. Nor could they afford to risk the wrath of the Roman cohorts, who had but scanty sympathy with their religious squabbles. Whatever they did would have to be done quickly, as the Passover and Sabbath were upon them, and that was the time to be religious! Nor were they sure where to find Him, as He had disappeared for the moment. It was a frustrating and exasperating situation. They were determined, however, that they would not rest until they had done away with Jesus.

Just at that point help came from a most unexpected source—from Judas, one of the Prophet's own disciples. "What will you give me if I deliver him unto you?" he said. And they struck up a bargain for thirty pieces of silver (about twenty dollars). From then on Judas sought opportunity to betray Him. Judas knew that Jesus spent many of His night hours in prayer out in the open. (Cf. Matthew 14:23; Mark 1:35; 6:46; Luke 5:16; 5:12; 9:18; 9:28; 11:1; etc.) He also knew pretty well where these places were. It remained only to know the right place at the right time. They had agreed on a means of identification. It was to be the symbol of love and friendship—a kiss!

Thus our Lord was betrayed by His prayer habits

—by one of those closest to Him—at the instigation of the highest religious leaders of His people! The crowning paradox and mystery is that it was all by the will of God almighty, the Father of love and of Jesus Christ! The mystery of Judas is a part of the mystery of all sin. Only one mystery is greater: the divine mystery of the atonement itself, and the love of Him who compelled even wicked and contemptible men to serve Him in solving the equation of sin! But woe unto them by whom the offense came! It were better for them if a millstone had been hung about their necks and they had been drowned in the depths of the sea; it were better for them if they had never been born!

Christ was identified by His prayer habits and His virtues. It would be well if we, too, could be identified and conspicuous because of our prayer habits and our life in Christ.

PRAYER

O Christ, our hope, our heart's desire, redemption's only spring! Creator of the world art Thou, its Savior and its King. How vast the mercy and the love which laid our sins on Thee, and led Thee to a cruel death, to set Thy people free. O may Thy mighty love prevail our sinful souls to spare! O may we come before Thy throne, and find acceptance there! Amen. Ancient Latin hymn

Anointed for death

As he sat at table, a woman came with an alabaster jar of ointment of pure nard, very costly, and she broke the jar and poured it over his head. . . . And they reproached her. But Jesus said, "Let her alone; why do you trouble her? She has done a beautiful thing to me. . . . She has done what she could; she has anointed my body beforehand for burying. And truly, I say to you, wherever the gospel is preached in the whole world, what she has done will be told in memory of her." Mark 14:3ff.

THIS scene seems to have taken place on Friday before Palm Sunday. All the Gospels tell of it, each in its own way omitting something or adding something. For this reason certain details and points of identification are not entirely clear. John adds (chapter 12) that the woman's name was Mary, and intimates that it might even have been Mary the sister of Martha. Another inference is that it was Mary Magdalene. An ancient tradition says

35

that she was the woman taken in adultery, in that much questioned passage, John 8. Whoever she was, it is enough to know that she was a lowly repentant sinner with a notorious past, whom Jesus had forgiven and raised from the gutter.

The setting is a banquet in the house of Simon at Bethany. If we read between the lines correctly, Jesus' enemies were there watching Him, and it was a coldly polite and formal scene. Then—here she comes, this street woman, right into their midst! It must be conceded that it was out of place and embarrassing, and that hers was a hysterical demonstration of ignorant, feminine emotionalism; and Judas doubtless had a point when he figured that sixty dollars' worth of cosmetics at one "sitting" was a waste of good money. And she was a real specimen of a sinner, a scarlet woman, albeit a humble and repentant one. How right they were, these coldly correct religionists, and yet how terribly and infinitely wrong!

Jesus was fully aware of all this, but He saw in her far more. He recognized the soul of a woman who had been rescued from perdition, repentant and humble and filled with gratitude. She gave a woman's gift, from the background of the kind of world she was most familiar with: cosmetics (nard), the most expensive that she could buy; the ancients drenched themselves with it. But she was not as grotesque in her devotion as her critics supposed, if we accept Luke's version as part of the same story. In those days a courteous host would welcome his guests with water and towel for their travel-stained feet and with oil for their hair, and a servant, too, to assist. Jesus Himself only a few nights later acted the part of that servant, in the Upper Room (John 13), when He took a towel and basin and washed His disciples' feet. But Jesus' host at Bethany did nothing. It is possible that this poor forgiven woman noted this, and tried in her way to make up for it. When she kneeled before Him and began to anoint Him in a confusion of tears and devotion, He understood and treated her with chivalry and kindness. "Let her alone!" He said. "She has done what she could."

Thank God for the condescension of the Savior toward all of us, both in our lack of devotion and in our maudlin excesses of it! This writer can not hold with those who would have us be cold formalists and who would banish from religion all enthusiasm, feeling and fervor. What a cold faith, cold liturgy, and cold experience this would make of the liveliest and most vibrant power in men's lives, their souls' contact with the Lord of Life!

Jesus praised her and declared that wherever the Gospel would be preached in times to come, she would be remembered and honored. And it is so. Then He added what none of them could have surmised: she had served God with her action, in that she had anointed Him for death. At His birth, kings had come from the east, and they had brought cosmetics too—frankincense and myrrh, fragrant and valuable products. Now for His death, she, the lowly one, emblematic of the sinners He came to save, brought a similar gift. It was not a cheap offering; it was costly, and its fragrance filled all the place, to remind them.

PRAYER

"Jesus sinners will receive" is the welcome news from heaven. He will anxious souls relieve, purge and cleanse them from sin's leaven. Burdened heart, hear and believe: Jesus sinners will receive!

From a hymn by ERDMANN NEUMEISTER, 1671-1756
Translation by H. E. JORGENSEN

We thank Thee, Lord, for Thy loving condescension toward the straying, no matter how lost and lowly we may be. Receive us all, we pray Thee, and lift us to some place at Thy feet. And when that great day comes, grant to us some humble place where we can see and hear Thee, way back, just inside the door, we who are so crude and clumsy and unused to the ways of the King! Give to us, too, who are of the great host of the illiterate and unwashed, to be numbered among the saved: Thou who didst walk and talk and mingle with the leprous and sin-branded, and love them, so long ago! Lord, remember us when Thou comest in Thy glory! Amen.

The man with the pitcher

And he sent two of his disciples, and said to them, "Go into the city, and a man carrying a jar of water will meet you; follow him, and wherever he enters, say to the householder, 'The Teacher says, Where is my guest room, where I am to eat the passover with my disciples?' And he will show you a large upper room furnished and ready; there prepare for us." And the disciples set out and went to the city, and found it as he had told them; and they prepared the passover. Mark 14:13-16

THE Passover was the chief of the national holy days of the Jews, for then they celebrated the birthday of their nation, in the liberation of the Israelites from slavery in Egypt way back in the days of Moses. The twelfth chapter of Exodus tells the story in detail. Every year they re-enacted symbolically the great event, in the preparation and eating of the Passover meal, and the observation of other rites in connection with it. This, then, was background and setting of that memorable Thursday night meeting of Holy Week, which ended with Gethsemane and Golgotha.

Jesus had longed for this meeting. But it had to be secret and secluded, lest it be discovered by His enemies and broken up before its purpose was accomplished. And this brings us to the "Man with the Pitcher." It was Peter and John who were sent to find and follow him. For a man to carry a water jar on the streets of Jerusalem was not a usual thing in Jesus' day, since it was the women who did that kind of chore work. But it did occasionally happen. A man, therefore, with a pitcher or jar of water on his shoulder or head would be conspicuous enough to attract attention, but not enough to excite suspicion or cause trouble. All went just as Jesus had said. Apparently there had been some pre-arrangement with Him, as there was no surprise when they entered the house and asked for the use of the guest chamber—it was ready for them.

It seems plausible, from a comparison of texts, that this same chamber was the gathering place of Jesus and His disciples after the resurrection until His ascension, and that they also continued to meet there until Pentecost, because it was secluded and safe from their enemies. Thus it came to have particularly holy memories, and was indeed the first church and sanctuary of that beginning-congregation of the New Testament.

It is not known who was "the man with the pitcher," or the host and owner of the house of the

Upper Chamber. But they have been symbolical ever since of lovers of the Lord, who have served Him humbly and been content to remain nameless, asking no acknowledgment, publicity, flattery, or praise. In every age, clime, and place where the Church has gone, they have played their part, even until our own day. Many a great and prosperous synod and congregation is proud to trace its beginnings to the help and home of some "man with a pitcher" or a host who opened his house to the first meetings where a church was born, little realizing what the Lord would cause to come of it. God bless the men with pitchers and open homes and hearts, who have played such humble and holy roles in the Mission History of the Church!

PRAYER

Christ, our great Passover, sacrificed for us: accept our humble thanks and the hospitality of our hearts! Prepare therein, we pray, a sacred Upper Chamber, so that we too can be near Thee and with Thee. Encourage us with assurance that the least small deed, done in devotion to Thee, is precious in Thy sight, and will be blessed. Thou for whom the greatest service in the world is but small, because all things are Thine, no gift have we! Amen.

And He took a towel

Jesus, knowing that the Father had given all things into his hands, and that he had come from God and was going to God, rose from supper, laid aside his garments, and girded himself with a towel. Then he poured water into a basin and began to wash the disciples' feet.   John 13:3-5

JESUS had longed for that last session with His disciples, with true longing. And His disciples needed it. There were still matters in regard to which they required briefing and reassurance. And surely, after all these months of experiences and holy companionship, there could be expected from these last moments special blessings and benefits that even the Lord Christ Himself was not above wanting and enjoying. With a kind of touching wistfulness He confided to them as they sat down together: "I have earnestly desired to eat this passover with you before I suffer; for I tell you I shall not eat it until it is fulfilled in the kingdom of God."

42

Surely it would be, throughout, an evening of never-to-be-forgotten fellowship and inspiration. Alas!

It started with a quarrel. They were arguing about who was to be regarded as the greatest among them. Then there was the episode of Judas, and Jesus' dismissal of him: "What thou doest, do quickly." And then the warning revelation: "Ye shall all deny me!" Jesus did not scold them or exclaim because of their quarrel about greatness. Instead He took a towel and a basin and went from one to the other, washing their feet, doing the task of the most menial servant. This act was far more powerful than any sermon or invective could have been. We may be sure that it was very quiet in the room by the time He was through. Only Peter objected, and he because he did not understand. "You shall never wash my feet!" he exclaimed. And Jesus replied, "If I do not wash you, you have no part in me." That was enough. "Lord, not my feet only, but my hands and my head!" Not least significant in this scene is the Gospel of John's introduction to it: "Jesus, knowing that the Father had given all things into His hands, and that He had come from God and was going to God, girded Himself with a towel." What an object lesson in laying aside His divinity for the role of humility! "Do you know what I have done to you," He asked when He had resumed His place at the table again. "You call me Teacher and Lord; and you are right, for so I am. If I then, your Lord and Teacher, have washed your feet, you also ought to wash one another's feet."

43

The old question arises: Who are the true heroes? Who is great? Is it not he that does the most good in the noblest and most unselfish way? And what is the hallmark of greatness? Is it not service to our fellow men, in the spirit of self-effacement and to the glory of God? Many a time Jesus had told them this, and acted it out in demonstration too, over and over again. But they were such dull pupils, and stubborn of mind; and their thoughts were of themselves and face-saving and glory and gain!

Well, let us turn the spotlight of self-examination on our own selves! Why is it so difficult to get rid of the egotism, the selfishness, the megalomania that beset so many, even among those who are named after Christ? From church leader to rank and file, it is found! Sometimes it is merely amusing, but actually it is tragic and unworthy. There is an instinct of ego and selfishness in every one of us, even in serving Christ, oftentimes, that is amazing—scheming and jockeying and quarreling for position and prestige and pelf and self!

PRAYER

Lord Christ, Thou who art at once divine King and Prince of humility: Have mercy on us and empty us out, that Thou mayest come in and take over! Amen.

Is it I, Lord?

*And as they were eating, he said, "Truly, I say to you, one
of you will betray me." And they were very sorrowful, and
began to say to him one after another, "Is it I, Lord?"*
                                                Matthew 26:21, 22

THEY were eating their Passover meal. Abrupt-
ly Jesus paused and said, "Truly I say to you,
one of you will betray me!" Shocked and sad, they
looked at one another and at Him, and began to
ask, "Is it I, Lord?" They were all guilty. But there
were especially two.

The first was that shifty-eyed one who had already
made his bargain to betray Him. To him He said,
"What you are going to do, do quickly." John's Gospel states that the others did not know why Jesus
said this to Judas. Matthew records: "It is he who
has dipped his hand in the dish with me." But they
were all doing that. John adds: "It is he to whom
I shall give this morsel when I have dipped it."

45

But this was said to John, who was closest to Him; the rest did not overhear it. Perhaps the point was lost in the excitement. But might it also have been purposely ambiguous, in that He was too loving, too proud, too chivalrous, too deeply hurt, to disclose the identity of His betrayer? Alas, it was to be a part of His suffering, and among the most torturing of all, to be betrayed by a friend—and with a kiss! Judas stole quietly out.

The other special one was Peter. How different was the answer that he got! "Simon, Simon, behold, Satan demanded to have you, that he might sift you as wheat. *But I have prayed for you that your faith may not fail.* And when you have turned again, strengthen your brethren." All this for Peter the fisherman—big, clumsy, impulsive Peter, who could be so crude at times, and was to deny his Lord that very night. Disgraceful! And yet what a difference! Why? Because there is forgiveness for every sin, where there is confession and repentance. Our Lord looked ahead and saw in advance the victory of love and the cross, and that in triumph He would claim Peter again on the other side. Poor Judas could have had it too. But he would not. His was the revulsion of despair, not repentance unto life.

It is our turn to ask: "Is it I, Lord?" And to hear His answer: "Thou hast said!" For we were there. And many a time we have betrayed Him by thoughtless word or no word at all, by careless attitude, disgraceful example, and downright sin. It is our turn to make our confession, to weep the tears of

46

Peter, and to pray Peter's prayer. But, thank God, we can also receive Peter's assurance from the Lord: "I have prayed for thee; I have died for thee!"

PRAYER

Have mercy on me, O God, according to thy steadfast love; according to thy abundant mercy blot out my transgressions. Wash me thoroughly from my iniquity, and cleanse me from my sin! For I know my transgressions, and my sin is ever before me. Against thee, thee only, have I sinned, and done that which is evil in thy sight, so that thou art justified in thy sentence and blameless in thy judgment. . . . Purge me with hyssop, and I shall be clean; wash me, and I shall be whiter than snow. Fill me with joy and gladness; let the bones which thou hast broken rejoice. Hide thy face from my sins, and blot out all my iniquities. . . . For thou hast no delight in sacrifice; were I to give a burnt offering, thou wouldst not be pleased. The sacrifice acceptable to God is a broken spirit; a broken and contrite heart, O God, thou wilt not despise. DAVID: Psalm 51

The vine and the branches

"As the branch cannot bear fruit by itself, unless it abides in the vine, neither can you, unless you abide in me. . . . Apart from me you can do nothing."　　　　　　　John 15:4, 5

THE ancients knew much about horticulture, including its practical, technical aspects—indeed probably more than many of us, with our super markets, can openers, deep freezes, and gadgets. Virgil, for instance, who was a farmer's son in the century before Jesus, refers with bucolic fervor to the idyllic pleasures of intensive farming in his famous *Eclogues* and *Georgics,* and in terms of technology too. To be sure, it was easy for him to twang his lyre and break forth into dithyrambs about the birds and the bees and turning the glebe, while slaves dug up rocks and weeds and did the heavy work. But the ancients' knowledge of techniques and phenomena was neither casual nor archaic; it included scientific pruning, pollination, tree grafting and cross-grafting. So when our Lord referred to vineyards and vine dressing, He was on ground familiar to all His listeners. Paul also, in the eleventh chapter of Romans, has an interesting simile based on orchards and tree grafting.

In Jesus' sermon, there were the vinedresser, the vine, the branches, and the fruit. "My Father is the vinedresser," He said. God is indeed the Creator, Owner, and Overseer of all, and takes a vital and continual interest in His vineyard. His human plantings He tends and prunes lovingly that they may bear more and better fruit. But there is a warning: He lops off branches too, and casts them away, and He even uproots whole trees!

"I am the vine and you are the branches," He continued. The Church and its parishes are still referred to as the Vineyard of Christ. As members thereof, it is a privilege and a thrill to know that we are parts of the great Body of Christ—a relationship as intimate as that between the branch and the vine. But the branch is not the same as the vine, any more than the part is the same as the whole. The branch therefore must not get notions about itself; it is subordinate and responsible to the Vine. Furthermore it must be in continuous, live contact with the Vine or it dies. The simile is for all of us who are members in Christ. We must keep in actual and vital contact with Him, if there are to be fruits or indeed if we are to survive at all. "He who abides in me and I in him, he it is that bears much fruit, for apart from me you can do nothing."

Our Lord laid down two alternatives. The first one: "If a man does not abide in me, he is cast forth as a branch and withers; and the branches are gathered, thrown into the fire, and burned." The second one: "If you abide in me, and my words abide in you, ask whatever you will, and it shall be done for you." This is a divine invitation to prayer and a promise to answer. What a partnership! Then He continued: "By this is my Father glorified, that you bear much fruit, and so prove to be my disciples. As the Father has loved me, so have I loved you; abide in my love." Then comes the glory! "These things I have spoken to you that my joy may be in you, and that your joy may be full!" On the eve of torment, with the circle of His enemies growing tighter, He could speak of joy as freely and confidently as that!

PRAYER

Dear heavenly Father, give us share and surety in that great joy which is in Christ. Keep us in living, loving contact with Him. Let sap and vitality flow from Him to us, and through us to all whose lives are touched by ours, that Christ may be served and glorified, and good may be done, and flowers and fruit flourish where before were weeds and fallow ground! Hear us in His name, as we read and ponder and pray! Amen.

Let not your hearts be troubled

Let not your hearts be troubled; believe in God, believe also in me. In my Father's house are many rooms; if it were not so, would I have told you that I go to prepare a place for you? And when I go and prepare a place for you, I will come again and will take you to myself, that where I am you may be also. John 14:1ff.

IT WOULD be difficult to find anywhere in the whole Bible words more fraught with comfort and strength than these. What wonders of peace and assurance they have wrought at sick bed and grave? No wonder they have been a favorite text for two thousand years!

The meeting in the Upper Room was drawing to a close. It had started at a low point, with quarreling. But Jesus had led them higher and higher, through example and admonition and vision and

51

prayer and holy Eucharist. They were sensing more and more clearly His references to suffering, separation, cross, and death. But the assurance and victory beyond they could not yet grasp, and a heavy feeling of dread hung over them. It was to this that He now addressed Himself.

Yes, it was true that there would be separation and suffering and death, for this was necessary according to the wisdom of God. But only for a short while, and then they would be together again in a new kind of union and victory that nothing could ever mar. The comfort in these words was not lost on them, but His references to the "little while" and the "long while," with death in between, confused and disturbed them. For death is a stubborn and real and permanent thing. This Jesus knew and gave them a promise: "These things I have spoken to you while I am still with you. But the Counselor, the Holy Spirit, whom the Father will send in my name, he will teach you all things and bring to your remembrance all that I have said to you." This was a prophecy and promise of Pentecost.

Again we come to the sermon application. Who will say that the distress of the disciples does not come very close to us too, even though the "little while" of Christ's cross and death is over and swallowed up in the "long while" of His victory and resurrection? But the fears and frustrations of life are plenty real to us also, and press in on all sides. And death is everywhere. So, then, to us too the Lord comes with His "Let not your hearts be troubled!" and His "Peace I leave with you; my peace I give to you; not as the world gives do I give to you. Let not your hearts be troubled, neither let them be afraid!" How precious are these words!

And where do we meet Him? In His written Word every time we open the book; in the spoken word every time it is preached according to Scripture; in the holy Sacrament every time we wait upon Him at the altar rail; in prayer and inner communion, of music or silence or whispered intercession. "For when we cry 'Abba, Father!' it is the Spirit himself bearing witness with our spirit that we are the children of God; and if children, then heirs, heirs of God and fellow heirs with Christ. Who shall separate us from the love of Christ? Shall tribulation or distress or famine or nakedness or peril or sword? No! in all these things we are more than conquerors through Him who loved us. For I am sure that neither death nor life, nor angels nor principalities, nor things present nor things to come, nor powers nor height nor depth nor anything else in all creation, will be able to separate us from the love of God in Christ Jesus our Lord!" (Romans 8.)

PRAYER

"Let not your hearts be troubled! Believe in God, believe also in me." We thank Thee, Lord Jesus! Amen.

Jesus prays for His own

When Jesus had spoken these words, he lifted up his eyes to heaven and said, "Father, the hour has come; glorify thy Son that thy Son may glorify thee. . . . I have given them the words which thou gavest me, and they have received them. . . . I am praying for them; . . . for they are thine . . . Holy Father, keep them in thy name . . . that they may be one, even as we are one . . . sanctify them in the truth; thy word is truth. . . . I do not pray for these only, but also for those who are to believe in me through their word . . . that the world may believe that thou hast sent me . . . and hast loved them even as thou hast loved me . . . that the love with which thou hast loved me may be in them, and I in them. John 17

WITH His enemies closing in on Him, and His friends about to run away, faced with scorn, scourging, and death, one might have expected our Lord to feel sorry for Himself and give vent to bitter denunciation of His enemies and scorching prophecies of their doom. At least, according to the custom of heroes and melodramatics, one might have expected some moments of self-praise and commiseration and strutting. Jesus did nothing of the sort! He referred to His enemies, but only casually; He referred to Judas also, but with sorrow as over a lost soul; of His defecting disciples He spoke with optimism and love. And He lifted His voice in prayer.

What a prayer! It is called "The High Priestly Prayer" and is the longest prayer recorded from the lips of the Savior. It covers everything essential to His Messiahship; the disciples are the object of most of it, and it dwells on the themes of glory and love. He speaks of the glory of God made manifest through the Son and His ministry; which is to be succeeded by the glory of the cross made manifest to all the world through the ministry of His disciples and their successors. So then it includes us also! What an impassioned pleading of love for those who were about to deny Him—that He might keep them and that through them testimony might be given through the preaching of the Gospel all down the ages. Only one He had to give up. It was Judas. "I have guarded them," Jesus pleaded with the Father, "and none of them is lost but the son of perdition, that the scripture might be fulfilled." The history of the Gospel and of the Church is compelling witness that Jesus' High Priestly Prayer was answered. It was a prayer of triumph!

What a pity that there are those who find it difficult to believe in prayer, even among those who recognize God! What a pity—not least in our own day, when two thousand years of history and the high advancement of our age have brought us into closer understanding of God and His wonders than ever! What a pity—since God has promised so much and anchored it to prayer!

If radio's slim fingers can pluck a melody
From night—and toss it over a continent or sea;
If the petalled white notes of a violin
Are blown across the mountains or the city's din;
If songs, like crimson roses, are culled from thin blue air—
Why should mortals wonder if God hears prayer?

ETHEL ROMIG FULLER, b. 1883

"Ask, and it will be given you; seek and you will find; knock, and it will be opened to you. For everyone who asks receives, and he who seeks finds, and to him who knocks it will be opened" (Matthew 7:7).

Every morning lean thine arms awhile
Upon the window-sill of heaven
And gaze upon thy Lord.
Then, with the vision in thy heart,
Turn strong to meet thy day.

AUTHOR UNKNOWN

PRAYER

Lord, teach us how to pray aright, with reverence and with fear; though dust and ashes in Thy sight, we may, we must draw near. We perish if we cease from prayer; O grant us power to pray, and when to meet Thee we prepare, Lord, meet us by the way! Amen.

JAMES MONTGOMERY, 1771-1854
"The Preparation of the Heart in Man"

56

In remembrance of me

As they were eating, Jesus took bread, and blessed, and broke it, and gave it to the disciples and said, "Take, eat; this is my body." And he took a cup, and when he had given thanks he gave it to them, saying, "Drink of it, all of you; for this is my blood of the covenant, which is poured out for many for the forgiveness of sins. . . . This do in remembrance of me." Matthew 26:26-28; Luke 22:20 and footnotes

THE high point of the evening of Holy Thursday was the institution of the Lord's Supper. To anyone who reads the Gospel records even casually, there can be no question as to the importance of this event. It is obvious that Jesus meant it to be the earnest and center of the New Testament covenant and the rallying place of the Church. More than that, it is evident from the texts that it is meant to be a Sacrament, a Means of Grace and bestower of the forgiveness of sins. The succeeding story of the Gospel and the Church also bears this out. (Cf. I Corinthians 10:16 and 21; 11:23-30; and the opening chapters of Acts.) Certain it is that of all the rites and privileges of a Christian, it is one of the most sacred and intimate.

Very simply the Lord proceeded. He took bread, blessed, brake it, and said, "Take, eat; this is my body." And He took the flagon of wine, thanked, and said, "Drink of it, all of you; this is my blood poured out for the forgiveness of sins." It is the analysts and arguers, and a certain type of theologian, that have complicated and muddled up this most precious of institutions. We ought not to rationalize the Lord's Supper, as some do. Nor is there any need to argue about the "real presence" of the Lord. One may call it mystic, sacramental, "under or over or in and through" the bread and the wine, or by any other term, but it seems impossible to read the words and texts and then deny the actuality and reality of His presence. We are not asked to understand or dissect that actuality—even Jesus did not stop to explain it—nor do we need to account for it. But we do not dare preach or commune with a divided Christ; and so, as with His miracles, we accept it in simple faith and with humble gratitude and joy.

Holy Communion is not a promiscuous or careless thing; it is the privilege of the repentant, the devout, and the sincere. All the Bible passages having to do with the Eucharist point to this fact, and the history of the early Church corroborates it. Paul, for instance, warns sternly against indiscriminate and non-discerning participation at the Lord's Table.

The Communion rail should therefore be maintained as a most holy place. But we are not permitted to stand guard precociously or with man-made rules, as policemen or dictators over God's free Means of Grace, lest we deny access to the Throne of Mercy. It is therefore regrettable that in certain circles there has occasionally been a kind of harsh belligerence in their very solicitude that has befuddled and scared away humble and seeking souls and withheld Christ's forgiveness and mercy. At the kneeling-rail of the Lord's Supper, sweet and fragrant with the mystic grace of His holy presence, and radiant with forgiving love and intimacy with the Savior— here have been the haven and harbor of rest and strength for Christ's redeemed all down the centuries. Let it remain that and not be an object of contention; let Holy Writ be taken at its word, untampered with and simple, and received with simple faith and gratitude. The bulk of the responsibility for error and transgression in attendance at Communion must ever rest squarely upon the communicant himself.

> According to Thy gracious word,
> In meek humility,
> This will I do, my dying Lord;
> I will remember Thee.
>
> Thy body, broken for my sake,
> My bread from heaven shall be:
> Thy testamental cup I take,
> And thus remember Thee.

Gethsemane can I forget?
Or there Thy conflict see,
Thine agony and bloody sweat,
And not remember Thee?

When to the cross I turn mine eyes,
And rest on Calvary,
O Lamb of God, my sacrifice,
I must remember Thee!

Remember Thee, and all Thy pains,
And all Thy love to me!
Yea, while a breath, a pulse remains,
Will I remember Thee.

And when these failing lips grow dumb,
And mind and memory flee,
When Thou shalt in Thy Kingdom come,
Then, Lord, remember me!

JAMES MONTGOMERY, 1771-1854
"I Will Remember Thee"

It seems very doubtful that Judas remained for the Lord's Supper. Surely he did not have the gall to do so! The Gospels of Matthew and Mark also indicate this. Luke (22:14-23) hints that the institution may have come first, but the text is not conclusive, and Luke's material is not always chronological in its arrangement. John does not include the institution of the Lord's Supper in His Gospel. But all the Gospels place the departure of Judas early in the evening; and this also fits best into the sequence and logic of events.

PRAYER BEFORE COMMUNION

O Lord, our God: We come before Thee as poor sinful beings, and are without excuse in that we have sinned against Thee by thought, word, and deed. But we believe in Thine only begotten Son, Jesus Christ, who hath suffered death for our salvation; and for His sake we pray Thee: Forgive us all our sins! Grant us Thy Holy Spirit, to the end that we may believe Thy pardoning Word, and that, according to the purpose and desire of our hearts, we may flee all sin and may suffer Thy holy and blessed will to rule in all things. Lord, have mercy upon us. Amen.

From the *Altar Book*

When they had sung a hymn

And when they had sung a hymn, they went out to the Mount of Olives.   Matthew 26:30

THE Gospels do not state what that hymn was. But it was undoubtedly the closing portion of the "Hallel Psalms" which were always sung during the Passover (Psalm 113 or 115 to Psalm 118). If so, it was with thoughts like the following that they left the Upper Room and braced themselves for what lay ahead. And truly, no more helpful or significant Psalm could have been chosen:

> O give thanks to the Lord, for he is good;
> His steadfast love endures for ever! . . .
> Out of my distress I called on the Lord;
> The Lord answered me and set me free.
> With the Lord on my side I do not fear.
> What can man do to me? . . .
> It is better to take refuge in the Lord
> Than to put confidence in man.

It is better to take refuge in the Lord
    Than to put confidence in princes.
All nations surrounded me; . . .
    In the name of the Lord I cut them off! . . .
I was pushed hard, so that I was falling,
    But the Lord helped me.
The Lord is my strength and my song;
    He has become my salvation . . .
I shall not die, but I shall live,
    and recount the deeds of the Lord. . . .
I thank thee that thou hast answered me
    And hast become my salvation.
The stone which the builders rejected
    Has become the chief corner-stone.
This is the Lord's doing;
    It is marvelous in our eyes. . . .
Save us, we beseech thee, O Lord!
    O Lord, we beseech thee, give us success! . . .
The Lord is God,
    and He has given us light. . . .
O give thanks to the Lord, for he is good;
    For his steadfast love endures for ever.
                                   Psalm 118

The Book of Psalms was Jesus' childhood hymnbook, and had been that of His people for a thousand years. He knew it by heart; His sermons and discourses were dotted with quotations from it; He fought the Evil One with its verses, at the time of His temptation in the wilderness; and now very soon He would be quoting it again from the cross in the agony and delirium of His suffering.

Who can estimate the power and importance of music! The world was created to the accompaniment of its power and rhythm, "when the morning stars sang together and all the sons of God shouted for joy!" (Job 38:7.) When our Lord was born at

Bethlehem, He was heralded with heavenly music: "And suddenly there was with the angel a multitude of the heavenly host praising God and saying,

> Glory be to God in the highest,
> And on earth peace among men
> With whom he is pleased!
>
> Luke 2:14

And when He returns to claim His own, and we begin eternity together, it will be with music. "Then I looked, and lo, on Mount Zion stood the Lamb. . . . And I heard a voice from heaven like the sound of many waters and like the sound of loud thunder; the voice I heard was like the sound of harpers playing on their harps, and they sing a new song before the throne and before the four living creatures and before the elders" (Revelation 14:1ff).

A MUSICIAN'S PRAYER

Heavenly Father, lay Thy cheek gently against my soul and being and draw with tender hand the violin-bow of Thy great compassion across these discordant trembling heartstrings of mine. Coax and tune them with Thine own dear hand, and teach them how to vibrate and sing eloquently and in tune with the harmony of Thy will and the beauty of holiness! Forgive my clumsy efforts to make music of my own without Thee; and be Thou my Teacher and Master and Guide, until I join those who stand before Thy throne, with golden, heavenly instruments in their hands, and the New Song on their lips, of praise and glory to the Lamb! Hear my humble plea, in the name of Him who through prayer and the chanting of a childhood hymn found strength to go on to Gethsemane and wrestle and bleed and die for our redemption! Amen.

Gethsemane

And He came out, and went, as was his custom, to the Mount of Olives to a place which was called Gethsemane ["Wine Press"] . . . and the disciples followed him.
                              Matthew 26:36; Luke 22:39

IT WAS late when the little group wound its way through the narrow streets of Jerusalem, out through one of its eastern gates, and down the slope and on until they came to a certain grove of olive trees. They had been there before and were familiar with the place. Behind them lay the great city, with lights still twinkling here and there as it settled down for the night. There somewhere were His enemies who would soon be upon Him. Above, to the east, slumbered the friendly little villages of Bethphage and Bethany, where Jesus and His disciples had found their kindliest hospitality during these grueling days.

Then, pausing as though struck by something, Jesus said to His disciples, "Sit here, while I go yonder and pray." And taking with Him only Peter and John and James, the Inner Three, He went on a little farther into the grove. Suddenly the agony of Gethsemane was upon Him. Like some wounded creature of the woodland, He tore Himself away from them and staggered on ahead among the trees. The next moment He was on the ground, writhing in pain, and praying: "My Father, if it be possible, let this cup pass from me!" but adding quickly, "Nevertheless, not as I will but as Thou wilt!" Then He came back to the three as though seeking strength and sympathy. They were sleeping. The tensions of the past days were too much for them, and their very sorrows had worn them out. There was a brief warning to watch and pray, particularly to Peter as the one who had boasted the most loudly. But He added, with that compassion that was so characteristic of Him: "The spirit indeed is willing, but the flesh is weak." He turned back; this was a battle that He would have to fight out alone!

A second time, like waves from hell, the agony was upon Him, and He prayed for release. But again there was strength to add: "Nevertheless, not my will but Thine be done!" His great Savior-heart pounded until the blood burst through the capillaries and the pores of His skin. Then, wet with sweat and beaded with blood, He returned to the three. Heavy with sleep and sorrow, they were as though drugged and knew not what to answer Him (Mark 14:40).

A third time Jesus tore Himself away in agony; and more earnestly than ever prayed the selfsame prayer. Then an angel from heaven came and strengthened Him, and the first round of the Battle of Redemption was over! There was to be one more experience of the Agony of the Lost; it would be while He was nailed to the cross. Jesus now returned for the third time to His disciples; this time He came with victory.

> Go to dark Gethsemane,
> Ye that feel the Tempter's power;
> Your Redeemer's conflict see,
> Watch with Him one bitter hour;
> Turn not from His griefs away,
> Learn of Jesus Christ to pray.
>
> JAMES MONTGOMERY, 1771-1854
> "Christ the Example"

PRAYER

When my love for God grows weak, when for deeper faith I seek, then in thought I go to thee, Garden of Gethsemane. There I walk amid the shades, while the lingering twilight fades; see that suffering, friendless One weeping, praying there alone. Then to life I turn again, learning all the worth of pain, learning all the might that lies in a full self-sacrifice.

J. R. WREFORD, 1837

I thank Thee, Lord, for that suffering, and the willingness of that suffering, that God and man might be reconciled and the debt of sin paid and cancelled forever! Help me to thank Thee in deed as well as in word, in a life of goodness and sacrifice and service to my fellowmen! Amen.

The arrest

While he was still speaking, Judas came, one of the twelve, and with him a great crowd with swords and clubs. . . . And he came up to Jesus and said, "Hail, Master!" and he kissed him. . . . Then they laid hands on Jesus and seized him.
Matthew 26:47ff.

THEY had not long to wait after Jesus' Passion in Gethsemane. Flickering lights were already beginning to appear, and the clank of armed men was heard. It was a motley mob, made up for the most part of rag and tag, but it was a formidable one at that, for Jesus' enemies had laid their plans well. They had been able to procure a detail of Roman soldiers to go with them, and at their head marched Judas. So that no mistake might be made in the darkness, they had agreed on a sign of identification. And what a sign—the kiss of friendship! Sadly Jesus reproached him: "Friend, would you betray the Son of man with a kiss?" Jesus would still have been Judas' friend!

At first there was a show of resistance; Peter, for instance, seized his sword and began to lay about him, cutting off the ear of one Malchus, the slave of the high priest. Let us honor Peter for at least starting to fulfill his boast of loyalty. But, as usual, he did not understand. Jesus, reaching out His hand, healed the wounded man, and then said, "No more of this! Put your sword back into its place; for all who take the sword will perish by the sword. Shall I not drink the cup which the Father has given me?"

Then, turning to the mob, He said, "Have you come out as against a robber, with swords and clubs, to capture him? Day after day, I sat in the temple teaching and you did not seize me! But this is your hour, and the power of darkness." The irony of it—a whole troop of professional soldiers, plus an armed mob, to arrest an unarmed man at prayer in the middle of the night, Him known as the Prince of Peace! "Whom do you seek?" He asked them, and when they replied, "Jesus of Nazareth," He said, "I am he." With these words His divinity reasserted itself and in their old fear of Him they fell back in confusion. But it was not for Himself that He contended, it was for His disciples. "Then let these men go," He said. As the true and good Shepherd, He defended His flock to the last. By this time all the courage of the disciples had ebbed away and they fled headlong in a panic.

But there was one who barely got away that night. It was a young bystander, whom only the Gospel of Mark mentions but does not name. Many scholars think it may have been Mark himself, the writer of the Gospel. Roused by the clatter of the mob and soldiers going past his home so late at night, he seems to have thrown around him the first garment he laid hands on, and with a young man's curiosity hurried after the crowd. But in the darkness and excitement, the soldiers laid hold on him too. Terror-stricken he fled, leaving his garment in their hands, and escaped clad only in his loin cloth.

So ended Gethsemane. The Man of Galilee was alone and in the power of His enemies.

PRAYER

Good Shepherd, Thou who didst stand between Thy sheep and the foe, and didst lay down Thy life for them and us: how can we thank Thee enough? Continue to stand between us and our enemies, we pray Thee. And when we are weak and cowardly and do not measure up as we ought, love us still, we pray, and do not deny us or leave us as we might so richly deserve! Give us stronger faith and greater courage for Thee and the right. Give us strength and persistence to stand up against our own weaknesses and the efforts of the Evil One. And help us to present a finer and nobler testimony before the world on behalf of Thee, our Lord and our Friend. Amen.

Trial before Annas

So the band of soldiers and their captain and the officers of the Jews seized Jesus and bound him. First they led him to Annas; for he was the father-in-law of Caiaphas, who was high priest that year.   John 18:12

A T THE so-called trial of Jesus, His enemies followed, in a sort of way, the formal procedure prescribed by law; not because they wanted to but because they had to. But the whole thing was so wormy with irregularities and skulduggery that they could just as well have murdered Him in cold blood with a dagger in His back. They had to act quickly because the Sabbath was upon them and its observance was very strict; it was bad enough that this thing was mixed up with the Passover! As a religious group heading up the religious set-up of their people, they could not afford to ignore the mores of the fathers. But they forgot the Commandment which says:

71

Thou shalt not kill! The Prophet had many friends who were capable of staging a powerful demonstration if they were given time to rally. So it was found expedient, though illegal, to act under cover of night and as soon as possible.

Accordingly, they rushed Jesus for a sort of preliminary hearing before Annas. Strictly speaking, he had no business sticking his nose into this affair, since he had no official status or connection with it; it was his son-in-law Caiaphas who was high priest that year and headed up the Jewish tribunal. But Annas was a foxy old villain, and although now seventy years old, still had his fingers in more pies than one. It was twenty years since he had himself been high priest; but he had engineered it so that five of his sons had had their turns at that lucrative position, and now his son-in-law had the job. Annas was still the power behind the throne, and there was not much that took place without him; thus it was important to have his endorsement. This was not difficult because he was already partner in their guilt.

When they arrived at his palace, Annas was still up and waiting for them. Together they made short shrift of the Prophet from Nazareth. With cold composure, the former high priest asked Jesus about His disciples and His teachings. He received an answer that rocked him and put himself under cross-examination: "I have spoken openly to the world; I have said nothing secretly. Why do you ask me? Ask those who have heard me, they know what I said to them." Then one of the officers struck Jesus with his hand,

72

saying, "Is that how you answer the high priest?" Jesus replied with dignity, "If I have spoken wrongly, bear witness to the wrong; but if I have spoken rightly, why do you strike me?"

All in all, Annas could not do much with this witness who turned the tables on him so quickly. He does not even seem to have given formal judgment in the case, but passed him on to his son-in-law and the Sanhedrin, or Jewish Senate, who were by now assembled and waiting. The first farce of Jesus' trial was over.

We soliloquize. Sometimes one gets tired of church history, and the intrigues of religious bodies after they have attained largeness and affluence and have arrived at wealth and pomp and gotten into politics and in league with this world. And one finds it hard not to conclude that no one group, not even the Church, is wise enough to take over the total affairs of men. Perhaps there is some kind of divine wisdom behind this that the Lord permits so many groups and denominations and divisions among us, so as to neutralize and balance one another! Perhaps this thought is just whimsy, but there are moments. . . .

PRAYER

Lord, let the Church be the Church! Give her courage not to conform to the ways of this world; but keep her on the beam, as the conscience of the nation, the promoter of culture and virtue, the rebuker of the sinner, the inspiration of the saints, and the faithful custodian of religious truth! Thy Word is truth. In the name of Him who said, "My Kingdom is not of this world," we pray. Amen.

Trial before Caiaphas

*Annas then sent him bound to Caiaphas to the high priest.
. . . Now the chief priests and the whole council sought false
testimony against Jesus that they might put him to death, but
they found none.* John 18:24; Matthew 26:59

THE Sanhedrin, before which Jesus now appeared, was what was left of the supreme tribunal of the Jewish nation. It consisted of seventy elders, plus the high priest, who was the president. Originally it had both secular and religious jurisdiction, but Rome had long before shorn it of its secular powers, including that of capital punishment. Therefore, to bring about Jesus' death, it was necessary to have confirmation of the Sanhedrin's sentence by the governer. And the dirty work of slaying Him would also have to be done by Rome. In this case it would be by crucifixion. In the present instance this was not easy to procure. There would be no use, for instance, in playing up the religious angle, as the Romans had only disdain for the religious squabbles of the Jews. The Sanhedrin met in the temple area itself. There had been times in the past when this body had had a dignified history of equitable procedure; but internal and external corruption had long ago taken care of that! Now the Sanhedrin sat mostly as a debating society, wordy and impotent, defending obsolete dogmas and ideologies, discussing endless minutiae, and arriving at nothing. Its meeting and procedure now at midnight were of course illegal and outrageous, in spite of efforts to appear technically correct.

When Jesus was pushed into their midst, Joseph Caiaphas was in the president's chair. The purpose of the session was not to sift evidence and arrive at an equitable decision; it was merely to give the appearance of legality to a murderous decision already agreed on. But even so, they were having a hard time of it. They had scoured the city for witnesses so as to procure a case, but when they got them together, all the bribery and briefing they could bring to bear could not get them to lie consistently, so much so that the whole affair threatened to become a fiasco. Finally they managed to produce two witnesses who testified: "This fellow said, 'I am able to destroy the temple of God and to build it in three days' " (according to Matthew 26:61); and "We heard him say, 'I will destroy this temple that is made with hands, and in three days I will build another not made with hands' " (according to Mark 14:58). They were evidently garbled or vicious versions of what Jesus had referred to in His discourses on two very separate things: the destruction of the temple and His own prophesied resurrection on the third day.

Meanwhile the Prisoner said not one word, insomuch that they marveled. "Have you no answer?" the high priest said to Him impatiently. And still He remained silent! The ramblings of these illiterate perjurers were unworthy of a reply. But was there not another reason? This had to go on; it was necessary as a part of the Mystery of the Atonement. This scene and subject have been the theme of many a song and hymn-prayer, from the lowly Negro spiritual, to Bach himself in his "St. Matthew Passion" oratorio. It was Jesus' patience and innocence!

> They crucified my Lord,
> And He never said a mumbalin' word!
> Not a word, not a word, not a word.
>
> They pierced Him in the side,
> And He never said a mumbalin' word!
> Not a word, not a word, not a word.
>
> He bowed His head and died,
> And He never said a mumbalin' word!
> Not a word, not a word, not a word.

Perhaps no one has sung it with more touching simplicity than Marian Anderson, in her "Eleven Great Spirituals" (Victor Red Seal Records, LRM). And perhaps no one has set it more grandly and with greater simplicity than Bach in his "St. Matthew Passion" oratorio.

PRAYER

"Ah, holy Jesus, how hast Thou offended, that man to judge Thee hath in hate pretended? By foes derided, by Thine own rejected, O most afflicted! Who was the guilty? Who brought this upon Thee? Alas, my treason, Jesus, hath undone Thee! 'Twas I, Lord Jesus, I it was denied Thee; I crucified Thee. For me, kind Jesus, since I cannot pay Thee, I do adore Thee, and will ever pray Thee: Think on Thy pity and Thy love unswerving, not my deserving. Amen.

Text and chorale used in Bach's "St. Matthew Passion"
Text by Johann Heermann (1585-1647)
Translated by Robert Bridges (1844-1930)
Melody by Johann Crüger (1598-1662)

Peter

And the Lord turned and looked at Peter. And Peter remembered. . . . And he went out and wept bitterly. Luke 22:61f.

A NOTHER figure was also on trial that night. It was Peter. After the panic in the Garden of Gethsemane, he and John had followed the crowd in the darkness to see what the end would be. Peter was as one distracted; he could not stay away, and he could not come along properly. When they got to the palace of the high priest, John, who seems to have been well known, walked right on into the inner court without being challenged; but Peter got no farther than the outer gate. A moment later John returned and got permission from the door-keeper to let him in. Peter found himself in a strange and mixed crowd. It was cold and they had built a little charcoal fire to keep off the chill. Peter, shivering with more than the cold, found a place at the edge of the group. Here, in the flickering light, the door maid spied him, stared at him a moment, and said, "You also were with the Nazarene." But he denied it, saying, "I neither know nor understand what you mean!" Uneasily he edged away toward the outer court. The first pre-dawn rooster had just crowed to herald the coming day. Shortly after, someone else recognized Peter and said, "You also are one of them." But Peter replied, "Man, I am not!" A little later, one of the slaves of the high priest, a kinsman of Malchus, whose ear Peter had cut off, said, "Did I not see you in the Garden with him?" Others, too, were beginning to accost him with statements like: "Certainly, you are also one of them, for your Galilean accent betrays you." Then Peter began to curse and swear, and maintain: "I do not know the man!" Again the cock crowed.

At that moment they were leading Jesus away to appear before Pilate, after having been brow-beaten and scourged. He turned His anguished, bloody face, and looked at Peter. Not a word did He speak; but the look was enough. All of a sudden Peter remembered how the Lord had said, "Before the cock crows twice, you will deny me thrice." The sneer of a bar-moll, the chance reference of a bystander, that was all it took—and Peter was once more back in the days of his coarse fisherman life and denied his Lord with oaths. The next moment, in an agony of remorse and shame, he rushed out into the night, weeping bitterly.

It is very easy to heap scorn on Peter the coward that night—perhaps too easy, for those who are busy every day denying Him, each one in his own way. Perhaps the better way is to remember him against the background of all his later life. Then, somehow, Peter's denial fades before the picture of the aged, lonely pilgrim, trudging with tired, steadfast feet along the highway of the imperial Caesars, toward Rome and a martyr's death. "The devil asked to have you," Jesus had said. "But I have prayed for you! When you have turned again, strengthen your brethren." Peter remembered those words of his Master too—remembered them through his tears, we may be sure. And they helped him through.

PRAYER

In the hour of trial, Jesus, plead for me
Lest by base denial I depart from Thee!
When Thou seest me waver, with a look recall,
Nor for fear or favor suffer me to fall!

JAMES MONTGOMERY (1771-1854).
"Original Hymns": "Prayers on Pilgrimage"

So Thou art a king, then?

Pilate entered the praetorium again and called Jesus, and said to him, "Are you the king of the Jews?" Jesus answered, "Do you say this of your own accord, or did others say it to you about me? . . . My kingship is not of this world . . ." Pilate said to him, "So you are a king?" John 18:33ff.

OF COURSE Jesus is King! What else could He be? He is more than a king, He is *the* King: King of kings and Lord of lords! Triumphantly Handel sings of Him in his famous "Hallelujah Chorus"

> And He shall reign for ever and ever!
> Hallelujah, Hallelujah, Hallelujah, Hallelujah!
> King of Kings and Lord of Lords!
> King of Kings and Lord of Lords!
> Hallelujah!
>
> From "The Messiah," No. 42
> Based on Revelation 19:6 and 16

But His Kingdom is not of this world. And they who have tried to make of Him a terrestrial, political monarch, have erred almost as grievously as those who would not have Him King at all!

81

How busy this world's rulers have been, trying to dethrone Him! It started with Herod, when our Lord came into the world, and a whole community had to sacrifice its babes to satisfy the jealousy of a crazed monarch (Matthew 2). And now, at His death, they were at it again: Pilate with his sarcasm about "The King of the Jews," and the leaders of Israel with the scourge and the cross. And has it not been so ever since? Ebb and flow, ebb and flow, the tide has beaten against Him.

But He is a hard king indeed to beat down, this Jesus! He has a thousand scepters, and ten thousand strategies, yet never a sword! Far is He from being expelled from the earth, this Christ of ours, either by the ravages of time or the efforts of men. His mementos and memory are everywhere: on the walls of churches and schools and court rooms, on the tops of steeples and belfries and in the bronze tongues of the bells; on mountain tops and in wayside shrines, He is there in statue and frieze and bust; over sick-beds and over tombs, His symbol and sign are there; in nursery and lobby and shop. Take away the frescoes from gallery and church, and the symbols from altar and window and font, and He is still there! He inspires artist and musician and poet. Throw away prayer books and postils and you have left millions of books in the literature of all times and people. Yes, a hard King to down, is Jesus of Nazareth! Scourging and ridicule will not do it, nor will fire and sword; too deeply is He enshrined in the hearts of His millions of followers in every age and place. And so will it be until the end of the earth. Every conqueror and thinker has bowed to Him, or will—from Napoleon to Stalin, from Karl Marx to Ingersoll. History is divided squarely by His name: it is B.C. and A.D., before Christ and after Him. Caesar was more talked of in his day, but Caesar is dead. Aristotle taught more science, but Aristotle is passé. Jesus is alive and lively! The very fury of so many against Him is proof that He is not dead; the very people who pass their lives in denying and defying Him, lend their raucous voices in keeping His name and fame alive before the world. Even the oaths of those who revile Him are witnesses to and a recognition of Him. Yes, Jesus is King, alive and lively!

In our day, too, His enemies are having their little fun at the sacrifice of their souls, and the contempt of those who will be reading their history afterward: atheistic communism, Societies of the Godless, and the Smart Alecks of certain circles in the world of humanistic educators. As an example of their gall and procedure among the common people of our own country, we quote from a poster which was distributed in one of our large California cities in November, 1940 (abbreviations and deletions are ours):

"ATTENTION CHRISTIANS!! Be sure to attend the $. . . . luncheon at . . . . Hotel, Friday, November 15th, 1940, at 12:15 promptly. Hear the distinguished young . . . . poet, ..., Author of the following poem, and member of the American section of Moscow's "International Union of Revolutionary Writers."

"GOODBYE CHRIST"

Listen, Christ,
You did alright in your day, I reckon—
But that day's gone now.
They ghosted you up a swell story too,
Called it Bible—
But it's dead now
The popes and preachers 've
Made too much money from it.
They've sold you to too many.

Kings, generals, robbers and killers—
Even to the Czar and the Cossacks,
Even to Rockefeller's church,
Even to THE SATURDAY EVENING POST.
You ain't no good no more.
They've pawned you
Till you've done wore out.

Goodbye,
Christ Jesus Lord God Jehovah,
Beat it in away from here now.
Make way for a new guy with no religion at all—
A real guy named
Marx Communist Lenin Peasant Stalin
   Worker ME—

I said, ME!

Go ahead on now,
You're getting in the way of things, Lord.
And please take Saint Gandhi with you when you
      go,
And Saint Pope Pius,
And Saint Aimie McPherson,
And big black Saint Becton
Of the Consecrated Dime.
And step on the gas, Christ!
The world is mine from now on—
Move!

84

Don't be so slow about movin'!
And nobody's gonna sell ME
To a king, or a general,
Or a millionaire.

"ATTEND THE LUNCHEON CHRISTIANS And hear . . . . and eat, *if you can.*" It is on a par with the insults and the scourging, that early Good Friday morning, April 7, 30 A.D. And what happened? Fifteen years after this insulting poster, the number of at least professing church members had gone up to ninety millions in our beloved America, and atheists and Smart Alecks were on the defensive; and Christ is King, as secure as ever in the hearts of His followers. Russia, too, will get tired of atheism, and Asia, and the societies of the godless the world over. Christ will outlive them all! "So Thou art a King, then?" The answer is YES!

PRAYER

O Jesus! King most wonderful, Thou Conqueror renowned;
Thou Sweetness most ineffable, in whom all joys are found!

When once Thou visitest the heart, then truth begins to shine:
Then earthly vanities depart, then kindles love divine.

May every heart confess Thy name, and ever Thee adore;
And, seeking Thee, itself inflame to seek Thee more and
    more! Amen.

BERNARD OF CLAIRVAUX (d. 1153)
(tr. Edward Caswall, 1849)

Before Pilate and Herod

*And Pilate said . . . "I find no crime in this man." . . . But
they were urgent, saying, "He stirs up the people, teaching
throughout all Judea, from Galilee even to this place." . . .
When Pilate . . . learned that he belonged to Herod's jurisdiction, he sent him over to Herod."*   Luke 23:4ff.

PILATE had now been governor of this part of
Palestine about four years. He had had rough
going from the start. What, between his own coarse,
headstrong nature and his sneering contempt for his
subjects, there were constant tensions and eruptions,
which he often put down with savage brutality. He
did not spend any more time in the capital city than
he had to, but preferred the seaside city of Caesarea.
When in Jerusalem, Pilate lived in a swanky palace
close by the temple area. In front of it was a large
tessellated square, called by the Jews "Gabbatha" or
"The Pavement." Since the governor was a Gentile
and a hated Roman besides, the Jews had religious

scruples about entering his premises; so this pavement became the meeting point when matters came up that touched upon these scruples. It doubtless irked the Roman snob no end to have to make such a concession to the Jews, but he had had enough experience with them by now not to incite them needlessly.

Disturbed at this early hour, it was with gruff words that Pilate asked what brought them there. A gruff question begets a gruff answer, and they replied, "If this man were not an evil-doer, we would not have handed him over!" "Take him yourselves and judge him!" Pilate retorted. They would certainly have done so gladly, but they had to remind him that that was not lawful. It did not take Pilate long to realize that the Nazarene was no crminal, that it was the mob he had to deal with. Their first accusation was: "We found this man perverting our nation!" But Pilate was not interested in their religious bickerings. Their second accusation was (of all things!) that Jesus was inciting the people not to pay tribute to Caesar. This lie was cut out of whole cloth, for only a short time before they had tried to trap Him on this very point, and He had given the famous answer: "Render to Caesar the things that are Caesar's, and to God the things that are God's." Pilate does not seem to have even bothered with this accusation; doubtless he saw through the hypocrisy of it. But he did realize that this rabble was out for the Prophet's blood, and that they were in an ugly mood. He could not afford to have too many "incidents" between him

87

and his troublesome subjects, for his was a political job and there were already enough stories seeping back to Rome to make him uneasy. But he held out still: "I find no crime in this man!" The mob was insistent. "He stirs up the people, teaching throughout Judea, from Galilee even to this place!" they yelled back. Their reference to Galilee gave Pilate an idea. Since that area was out of his jurisdiction and belonged to Herod, here was a chance to get rid of the whole mess. As it happened, Herod was even in Jerusalem these very days. So Jesus was pushed over to him.

Herod was right glad to see this famous prisoner, for he was curious to have Him perform some of His miracles for him. But it was a tame and disappointing interview; the Master said not one word! This little exchange, however, became a sort of bridge of reconciliation between the two governors, for they had not been on the best of terms lately. Accordingly, Jesus was once more led back to Pilate, the mob following as blood-thirsty as ever.

PRAYER

I see the crowd in Pilate's hall, I mark their wrathful mien; their shouts of "Crucify!" appall, with blasphemy between. And of that shouting multitude, I feel that I am one. And in that din of voices rude, I recognize my own.

Horatius Bonar, 1808-1889—" 'Twas I That Did It"

Lord, forgive my share of guilt that made Thee suffer so! Amen.

Pilate washes his hands

Pilate said . . . "Whom do you want me to release for you, Barabbas or Jesus? . . ." And they said, "Barabbas." Pilate said, "Then what shall I do with Jesus?" They all said, "Let him be crucified." . . . Pilate took water and washed his hands . . . saying, "I am innocent of this man's blood; see to it yourselves." And all the people answered, "His blood be on us and our children!" Matthew 27:15ff.

WE MOVE up to the final phase of Jesus' trial. Once more Pilate faced the mob and declared that both he and Herod had found nothing criminal about the prisoner. "I will therefore chastise him and release him," he said. But the beating up of an innocent man was not enough for them. Furiously they shouted: "Crucify him! Crucify him!"

Pilate tried again. There was a curious (and surely dangerous) custom of releasing at the yearly Passover one prisoner of the people's own choice, as a sort of gift to heighten the festivities. Pilate doubtless reasoned that if he offered them a choice between the Prophet and the most notorious criminal he had on his hands, they would choose the Nazarene. Barabbas, convicted of treason and murder, was just such a one. Pilate still shrank from permitting this innocent Prophet to be slain at the hands of a mob. Furthermore, he had just received a message from his wife: "Have nothing to do with that righteous man, for I have suffered much over him today in a dream!" But his idea with Barabbas was a vain and naive one. A furious clamor greeted it: "Not this man, but Barabbas!" they yelled

Once more Pilate tried. Perhaps if he had Jesus thoroughly scourged, the mob would be mollified by the sight, and he would at least save His life—it was better to be beaten than to die! So the soldiers stripped Jesus of His clothing and beat Him with whips. They made up a game. They plaited a crown of thorns and pressed it upon His head; they put a reed in His hand for a scepter; they threw over Him a purple robe, the symbol of royalty; and then, between bloody strokes, they mocked Him, saying: "Hail, King of the Jews!" Then, blindfolding Him, they struck Him again, saying: "Prophesy, who is it that struck you?" Finally, tired of the sport, they led Him, bloody and staggering, out before the people. Even Pilate, hardened as he was to such scenes, could not help exclaiming, "Ecce homo!": "Behold the man!"

But the mob was not mollified. Instead they shouted, "If you release this man, you are not Caesar's friend!" Mockingly but now much alarmed, Herod replied, "Shall I crucify your king?" And the chief priests answered, "We have no king but Caesar." We have come to one of the most dramatic and infamous moments in history. Obsequiously, Pilate called for a basin of water, washed his hands before them, and said, "I am innocent of this man's blood; see to it yourselves!" And all the people shouted, "His blood be on us and our children!" Then Barabbas was released and Jesus was ordered to be crucified.

No, Pilate, you will never wash your hands of that blood. The sea itself could never do it! Your name is engraved as in granite in the annals of infamy because of your deed; it is imbedded in our very Creed as an everlasting reminder—"crucified under Pontius Pilate." You are down forever as one of the monsters of history.

Out, damned spot, out I say! What? Will these hands ne'er be clean? Here's the smell of blood still; all the perfumes of Arabia will not sweeten this hand! Oh! Oh! Oh!"
Shakespeare's "Macbeth," Act V, Scene 1. Lady Macbeth

PRAYER — CONFESSION

Pilate, Pilate, wash your hands! Cry "What is Truth!" again. None asks or cares, those wiser days, nor fears so small a stain.

Peter, Peter, save your skin! Then, futile, weep your shame. No one will notice—after all, we have done the same.

Judas, Judas, hang yourself! How many times is this? The lesson's yet to learn—we still betray Him with a kiss.

Jesus, Jesus, nailed on high, Christ whom the nations praise! Which is the cross that tore Thee most, Golgotha's or today's?
ADA JACKSON, contemporary American poetess

The mystery of Judas

When Judas, his betrayer, saw that he was condemned, he repented and brought back the thirty pieces of silver . . . saying, "I have sinned in betraying innocent blood." And throwing down the pieces of silver he departed; and he went and hanged himself.   Matthew 27:3-5

THE most pitiable figure in the Passion history is Judas. ("Iscariot" probably means "the man from Kerioth.") He was the son of Simon of Kerioth (John 6:71), and the name would imply that he came of good stock. Somewhere along the way Jesus of Nazareth crossed his path, and Judas was impressed and cast in his lot with Him. He advanced to the point of becoming one of the Twelve and was chosen to be their treasurer. It is here that the mystery begins. The Gospels refer to him early as the betrayer (John 6:70, etc.), and to the fact that he would steal from their meager funds on occasion. All this the

Lord must have known from the very start, and yet He chose Judas and put up with him. Why? And with their ideologies so far apart, what did Judas see in Jesus that he should join his life with His? Perhaps for somewhat the same reason that some folks today join churches—for what they can get out of it.

When did the point of Judas' departure and repudiation come? There was a time when others, too, were leaving the Master (John 6), to such an extent that the Lord turned to His disciples and said sorrowfully, "Will you also go away?" And Peter made that good answer: "Lord, to whom shall we go? You have the words of eternal life!" Was that the turning point for Judas? But that he should actually betray Him, and for a paltry sum of money!

The mystery of Judas is a part of the terrible mystery of sin. Why should anyone choose sin in preference to goodness and the Christ? And yet great masses of people do so deliberately every day. A surge of pity, as well as abhorrence, comes over a Christian as he reads the story of Judas. The disciples always referred to him with a sort of horror, as the one who betrayed his Lord, "and went to his place." What place? Was his remorse only unto death, thus making it impossible for the saving love of Christ to reach him? The Bible gives but little encouragement.

The chief priests, picking up the pieces of silver, decided not to put it into the sacred treasury, since it was blood money. So they used it to buy a worn-out clay pit that had been a potter's field, and made it a burial ground for strangers and the poor. Long afterward Christians were still pointing it out, and referred to it as "Akeldama," "The Place of Blood." And to this day that section of many cemeteries where the bones of nameless transients, no-accounts, and the destitute are laid away at public expense, is referred to as "The Potter's Field."

Surely the terrible story of Judas holds lessons for all of us to watch and pray. The devil still goes about like a roaring lion, seeking whom he may devour. All sin is betrayal and is unto death, for the wages of sin is death. Let him that standeth take heed lest he fall!

PRAYER

O sacred Head now wounded, with grief and shame weighed down, now scornfully surrounded with thorns, Thine only crown; O sacred Head, what glory, what bliss, till now was Thine! Yet, though despised and gory, I joy to call Thee mine! Be near me when I'm dying; O show Thy cross to me! And to my succor flying, come, Lord, and set me free! These eyes, new faith receiving, from Jesus shall not move; for he who dies believing, dies safely through Thy love.

Ascribed to BERNARD OF CLAIRVAUX (1091-1153); translated freely by Paul Gerhardt (1607-1676) into German, and from thence into English by James W. Alexander, 1830

Via Dolorosa

And as they led him away, they seized one Simon of Cyrene,
who was coming in from the country, and laid on him the
cross, to carry it behind Jesus. And there followed him a
great multitude of the people, and of women who bewailed
and lamented him. . . . Two others also, who were criminals,
were led away to be put to death with him.   Luke 23:26ff.

THE tragic procession set out. According to law,
the crucifixion had to be outside of city limits.
It does not matter where that place was, whether the
site usually pointed out to tourists, or the more re-
cently proposed one known as "Gordon's Calvary,"
just northeast of Jerusalem. The Hill of Crucifixion
was a barren, forbidding knoll, having such resem-
blance to a human skull that it was called, in Hebrew
"Golgotha," in Greek "Cranium," and in Latin "Calvary"—all of which words mean "a skull." At the head
marched a sort of herald, carrying the superscription

that would be nailed to the top of each cross, explaining the crime of each. After him came the centurion in charge of the soldiers; after him, the victims, surrounded and preceded by soldiers; and after them, the crowd. The centurion has been given the name Longinus by tradition, which also adds that he became a believer that day, and later bishop of Cappadocia, south of the Black Sea.

Part of the cruelty of crucifixion was that the victim had to carry his own cross, if he had enough strength left to do so. But our Lord, worn out with sleeplessness and brutality, stumbled and fell under His heavy burden, and the soldiers had to lay hold on a spectator, a rugged young countryman named Simon of Cyrene, and force him to carry the cross, behind Jesus. And thereby they made him famous forever! As with Longinus, the crucifixion made such an impression on Simon that he, too, became a believer that day. He is usually identified with the father of Rufus and Alexander, who were later prominent members of the early Church (cf. Mark 15:21; Acts 19:33; and Rom. 16:13). They were no doubt unique and famous, and proud of the honor of being sons of him who had helped carry the cross of the Savior.

As might be expected, the sight of the procession drew a crowd that gazed at the spectacle with varied reactions. Somewhere not far off were Jesus' disciples, we know, and many others who had learned to love Him; and also that little band of faithful women, including His own mother, that had followed Him from Galilee and ministered to His daily wants. They wept in helplessness and sympathy as they watched the cruel scene. To them Jesus turned and said, "Daughters of Jerusalem, do not weep for me, but for yourselves and your children! For the days are coming when they will say, 'Blessed are the barren and the wombs that never bore!' and to the mountains, 'Fall on us!' and to the hills, 'Cover us!'" The prophecy of Jesus was sure. In His mind's eye He saw the horror that would descend upon the city, in God's great Day of Visitation, and upon the nation that refused to accept its Messiah, and laid violent hands on the Lord's Anointed!

PRAYER

We bless Thee, Jesus Christ, our Lord! Forever be Thy Name adored! For Thou, the sinless one, hast died that sinners might be justified. From sin and shame defend us still, and work in us Thy steadfast will, the cross with patience to sustain, and bravely bear its utmost pain. In Thee we trust, in Thee alone; for Thou forsakest not Thine own; to all the meek Thy strength is given, who by Thy cross ascend to heaven. Amen.

C. VISCHER, 1597

The crucifixion

And they brought him to the place called Golgotha . . . and
they crucified him. . . . And with him they crucified two
robbers, one on his right and one on his left. . . . And it was
the third hour, when they crucified him.   Mark 15:22ff.

THE CROSS

Lovely little symbol on a long lapel,
Or dangling from a golden chain about the neck,
Or maybe bigger, bolder, burnished—on a stand.
Improper art, in more than three ways wrong!
Wrong sizes—the cross is bigger than a well-fed man.
And heavy—more than one can carry all alone.
Wrong places—the cross is rightly worn upon the back.
Wrong finish—the cross is rough, with ugly splinters all along.

DAN WEST

CRUCIFIXION was a comparatively new form of torture in Jesus' day. It did not originate with the Jews, who preferred to stone or behead their criminals; it was Roman. The first crosses seem to have been the so-called "Tau" cross, in the form of a

"T", and the victim was tied with his back to it and his arms hung over the top. To prevent the body from sagging, a sort of podium, or support for the feet, was later added. After a while someone invented the torture of nails, and then the cross was complete for its devilish purpose.

When the procession arrived at Golgotha, the soldiers went quickly and methodically to work. They had several victims to dispose of, and the next day was the Sabbath, which began at sundown the evening before. The three crosses were laid on the ground, the condemned were forced to stretch themselves upon them, and then the vigorous stroke of hammers was heard as the nails were driven through quivering flesh, while the blood spurted. There had been some trouble about the superscription for the central cross. Pilate had ordered it inscribed "King of the Jews," in a sort of ribald continuation of the game they had played during the scourging of Jesus. It was printed in three languages: Hebrew, the language of religion; Greek, the language of culture; and Latin, the language of the court. Jewish leaders had kicked up quite a fuss about it, and urged: "Write not 'This is the King of the Jews,' but that he *said* 'I am the King of the Jews.'" But Pilate was tired of their wrangling and answered curtly, "Quod scripsi, scripsi!": "What I have written, I have written," and with that they had to be content. Finally there was a sickening thud, as each cross was raised and dropped into its hole, and the job was done!

They set the cross upon a hill,
And led Him forth to die;
And while the wondering heavens stood still,
They nailed the Christ on high!

From an ancient Greek hymn

Then they sat or stood around and watched Him—
the soldiers, the crowd, the Jewish leaders, the disciples, the women, all history, and you and I!

Many were the wise-cracks, ribald jokes, and twist-
ed contortions of what Jesus had said in His discourses, that were bandied about as they watched.
"You who would destroy the temple and build it in
three days, save yourself! . . . If you are the Son of
God, come down from the cross! . . . He saved others,
himself he can not save! . . . Let him come down
now from the cross and we will believe in him!"

And so they watched and listened and waited for
Him to cry out, or say something—and then die!

Upon a hill called Calvary,
A Man went forth to die;
He gave His body to a cross,
They built it huge and high.
They sent Him to oblivion (they thought)
With many a cruel cry!

Long years have passed since Calvary,
Those cruel cries are dead!
Dead, too, the hands that pressed the thorns
In torture on His head;
All gone into oblivion!
He is alive instead.

Ascribed to "R. S. C."

100

The seamless robe

And when they had crucified him, they divided his garments among them by casting lots; then they sat down and kept watch over him there. Matthew 27:35f.

THE soldiers, too, were having their little fun that morning. More stolid than the others, they did their job, took up their stations, and settled down to wait. To while away their time, they busied themselves with that ancient avocation of many a soldier (and others too) before their time and after—petty gambling. Roman custom gave to those presiding at an execution the hangman's privilege of keeping for themselves the clothing and other small personal belongings left by the victim. John's Gospel intimates that four soldiers were assigned to guard each of the crosses. Those in charge of Jesus took His garments and made four parts, one for each soldier. But His tunic was without seam, being woven from top to

101

bottom, likely hand-woven by some devoted follower, or even His own mother. "Let us not tear it," they said to one another, "but cast lots for it to see whose it shall be." And so they did. But they who shook dice for Jesus' seamless robe that day did not know that they were fulfilling Scripture! The same Psalm (22:16) that our Lord quoted in His terrible cry from the cross, "My God, my God, why hast Thou forsaken me?" contains also another passage pertinent to the scene, and the Gospel of John calls attention to it (19:24): "A company of evil-doers encircle me; they have pierced my hands and feet; they stare and gloat over me; they divide my garments among them, and for my raiment they cast lots."

It is curious and impressive to note how many of the incidents of the Passion story took place in literal and even minute fulfillment of Old Testament Scripture. Without knowing it, Jesus' enemies as well as His followers, fulfilled prophecies made many centuries before, in the poetry of the Psalms and the oracles of the prophets. Doubtless we, too, shall know some day how the villains, big and little, of our own times, the dictators, the killers, the strutters, who imagined in their conceit and folly that they were writing history in their own way, were in reality following the permissives or behests of God almighty instead. For a little while He uses them, after which He spews them out and gets rid of them. Even the petty soldiers under the cross are a confirmation of the fact that God's Word abides forever, and that He is the writer of history and in complete mastery of all that He has created, even to the smallest detail! "Thus far shall you come, and no farther; and here shall your proud waves be stayed" (Job 38:11).

So then, let us who worry and fret in our day, wondering whether the Almighty has any power or prerogatives left, let us be comforted and learn to trust Him completely in little things and in large—in our own little lives, in the history being written in our times, in the laws and convulsions of nature and of men, and in the whir of the atom and the whirl of the stars!

PRAYER

Thou, Jesus, whose Robe of Righteousness must be worn if we are to be saved—that precious garment of Thine own bestowal—we who stand as lowly as the lowliest wretch and heathen beneath Thy cross, pray Thee at the parting of Thy garments: give us a share too! We ask for Thy Robe of Righteousness! And this we ask: Give us Thy sandals, too, Lord, those holy, dusty sandals, stone-bruised and worn by errands of love! And teach us how to wear them, in services of love, all through a life-journey of virtuous living, Christly thinking, and daily helpfulness to our fellow men! In this bewildered, soul-starved generation of ours, give us Thy sandals, we pray Thee, while we are all on the way together. Hear us, loving, forgiving Jesus! Amen.

The seven last words

INTRODUCTION

All the ends of the earth shall remember and turn to the Lord; and all the families of the nations shall worship before him. . . . Posterity shall serve him; men shall tell of the Lord to the coming generation, and proclaim his deliverance to a people yet unborn, that he has wrought it.   Psalm 22:27ff.

AGAIN the text is from that great and terrible Twenty-second Psalm that our Lord quoted in agony from the cross; it is a fit conclusion to that Messianic Psalm.

How often, when dear ones die, we strain our ears to catch their last whispered words so as to treasure them in our hearts, and for assurance and strength, especially if we have cause to wonder: "Were they alright with God, were they at peace with Him when they left this earth?" And in the long silence of their absence we go back over what they said, and repeat it fondly to one another: "This was the last thing he did; these were the last words she spoke." Many a mother or sweetheart or spouse who has wor-

104

ried about the life and spiritual condition of some wayward one has received comfort and hope from what has been confessed and prayed and expressed during those last moments. And some, alas, have received none at all!

At the end of the journey of life, when one comes to the crossing of the Great Dark River, it would be reasonable to expect, of those still in possession of their wits and consciousness, that this would be a time for reverence and confession and reconciliation with God. And yet there have been those who have crossed over with the same levity, the same profane or cynical attitude with which they have lived. The last words of those who die can reveal much. The truth of this may be readily seen when we scan any list of "famous last words" of the great or the notorious down the years of the past, and lay it against the years and patterns of their lives.

For instance, in the following list, one does not need to vouch for all the examples, but they bring out the point. Beethoven, the irascible musician, roused in his last moments by a crash of thunder, sat up in bed, shook his fist at the heavens, and died. Goethe, the great questioner, exclaimed, "More light! More light!" But Joseph Addison, the cultured literary stylist, said, "See in what peace a Christian dies!"

Hobbes, the materialistic philosopher, confessed, "Now I am about to take my last voyage, a great leap in the dark." James V of Scotland quipped, "It came with a lass and will go out with a lass." But Sidney, betrayed to death, said, "I know that my Redeemer liveth!" Queen Elizabeth I, of England, exclaimed, "All that I have or have ever done, for just one more moment of time!" And Mirabeau, the ruthless revolutionist, "Let me die to the sounds of delicious music!"

John Knox, the preacher said, "Now it has come! My Lord, I am ready." Said Rabelais, the lewd writer of burlesque, "Let down the curtain, the farce is over!" And Talma, the actor, "The worst is that I can not see!" But Tasso the poet, and Charlemagne the Emperor, repentant on their death beds, said in the words of their Savior, "Lord, into Thy hands I commend my spirit." And Stephen the Martyr, as they stoned him, "Lord Jesus, receive my spirit" and, "Lord, do not hold this sin against them!" Thus men have died.

It is not strange that the last words of the Savior have been so meticulously and devoutly studied, both those at the time of His ascension, namely the Great Commission, and those from the cross. From the cross they add up to seven "words" or sentences, known as "The Seven Last Words." No phrases in all history have received the devotion and attention that these have had. Musicians have worked with them in all ages, from Schutz and Haydn, to Gounod and Stainer and Dubois; and writers and preachers innumerable have used them as themes for two thousand years. They have been venerated and memorized and quoted by countless millions of His followers; and no death bed scene is complete without at least one quotation from the cross.

And as Moses lifted up the serpent in the wilderness, so must the Son of man be lifted up, that whoever believes in him may have eternal life. For God so loved the world that he gave his only Son, that whoever believes in him should not perish but have eternal life.

John 3:14-16, ending in "The Little Bible."

Holy Jesu, by Thy Passion,
By the woes which none can share,
Borne in more than kingly fashion,
By Thy love beyond compare:
   Crucified, I turn to Thee,
   Son of Mary, plead for me.

By the Spirit, which could render
Love for hate and good for ill,
By the mercy, sweet and tender,
Poured upon Thy murderers still:
   Crucified, I turn to Thee,
   Son of Mary, plead for me.

Litany of the Passion,
from "The Crucifixion" oratorio (1887)
by John Stainer (1840-1901)

PRAYER

Thou art the Way, to Thee alone from sin and death we flee;
And he who would the Father seek, must seek Him, Lord, by Thee.
Thou art the Truth, Thy Word alone true wisdom can impart;
Thou only canst inform the mind, and purify the heart.
Thou art the Life, the rending tomb proclaims Thy conquering arm;
And those who put their trust in Thee, nor death nor hell shall harm.
Thou art the Way, the Truth, the Life; grant us that Way to know,
That Truth to keep, that Life to win, whose joys eternal flow.
   Amen.   GEORGE WASHINGTON DOANE, 1799-1859

107

Father, forgive them

THE SEVEN LAST WORDS · FIRST WORD

Father, forgive them; for they know not what they do.
Luke 23:34

CRUCIFIXION was a horrible means of death; the victims usually lingered a long time. Blistered by the sun, with their bloated wounds beset by flies, their screams could often be heard afar off until finally unconsciousness and death put an end to their misery. We know that with our Lord there was more than that! For by the mystery of the atonement, there was added His vicarious suffering for the sins of the world, and that was far beyond the pains inflicted by His Good Friday tormentors. His whole body ached for rest and death, which He resisted with all His might; for had He not dedicated His life to this moment, and did He not volunteer to suffer as much as was needful, to the very last, that others might find rest and peace in their hour of death? The revilings of at least one of His companions was already being heard. But He who had been quiet so much of the time through His trial and scourging, what would He have to say now in His last extremity? They waited for His words.

Finally they came. But how different from what they might have expected! From the depths of His soul, like a song of victory over torn flesh and weariness, came a prayer—not as from a creature to his God, but as of Son to Father: "Father, forgive them, for they know not what they do!"

No more sublime prayer was ever breathed than that since men began to pray! And they who find it difficult to forgive the errors even of the innocent, can well stand in awe of this prayer for the guilty who were busy that very moment putting Him to death!

Christ had, many times over, taught His followers both the prayer and the act of forgiveness, and even conditioned their own forgiveness upon it. "And forgive us our trespasses as we also forgive those who trespass against us." He had said in the Lord's Prayer; and so also in others of his discourses. His behavior now on the cross was the supreme test of His doctrine, His sermons, and His love. And divinely did He meet that test all the way to the end. How that prayer has rung round the world ever since, to bring sinners to repentance and tears of gratitude to the redeemed! How the world stands in need of that prayer now! And how we do, who write and read these words! For we are the ultimate cause and object of that prayer.

Jesus' prayer is our example; for no greater virtue can be shown by a Christian than to ask forgiveness for those who have not sought it, may not be aware of it, and may not even desire it or care! Forgiveness is wrapped up in mercy and sealed with love.

> The quality of mercy is not strained,
> It droppeth as the gentle rain from heaven
> Upon the place beneath; it is twice blessed:
> It blesses him that gives, and him that takes.
> 'Tis mightiest in the mightiest, it becomes
> The throned monarch better than his crown.
> His scepter shows the force of temporal power,
> The attribute to awe and majesty,
> Wherein doth sit the dread and fear of kings;
> But mercy is above this sceptered sway,
> It is enthroned in the hearts of kings,
> It is an attribute to God Himself,
> And earthly power doth then show likest God's
> When mercy seasons justice.
>
> > Shakespeare (1564-1616). "The Merchant of Venice." Portia's speech in Act IV, Scene 1

But God's mercy in Christ is far more than "tempered justice" followed by a court sentence, as in Portia's famous panegyric. It is followed by forgiveness, and forgiveness is cancellation.

PRAYER

When all Thy mercies, O my God, my rising soul surveys, transported with the view, I'm lost in wonder, love, and praise.

When nature fails, and day and night divide Thy works no more, my ever grateful heart, O Lord, Thy mercy shall adore!

JOSEPH ADDISON (1672-1719)

110

Today you will be with me in paradise

THE SEVEN LAST WORDS · SECOND WORD

Truly, I say to you, today you will be with me in Paradise.
Luke 23:43

A ND the robbers who were crucified with him also reviled him, we are told by Matthew and Mark in their Gospels. At least they both started to revile Him. But the innocence and divinity of that Mysterious One in the center—and that prayer of His —were too much for one of the robbers. He stopped short and rebuked his companion sternly: "Do you not fear God, since you are in the same sentence of condemnation? And we indeed justly; for we are receiving the due reward of our deeds. But this man has done nothing wrong." Then, addressing himself to Jesus, he prayed: "Remember me when you come in your kingly power!" This robber has been given the name of Dysmas (or Dismas) by tradition, and

111

has come down in history as "The Good Thief." The question could doubtless be raised: Is there such a thing as a *good* thief? And the answer would have to be No. But there are repentant and forgiven thieves. The question still remains: Who is good? It is a relative term only.

Quickly, clearly, and with finality, the answer to his prayer came back, "Truly I say to you: Today you will be with me in Paradise!" Jesus had just prayed: "Father, forgive!" Now He put it into action. One more conversion, one more soul for the Gospel net, before He bowed His head in death! Nor was He through even then! If the Bible passages concerning Simon of Cyrene are correctly understood, he may already have been converted; but there was yet one, the captain of the guard, who was also to become a convert that day—perhaps he was already struggling with his soul, as a result of that same prayer: "Father, forgive!"

The text of the Penitent Thief is one of the most glorious in the whole Bible. What a comfort it has been to many a dying wretch who has wasted his life in sin, and finds himself at the brink of eternity without peace with God! What assurance it has been to those who wake up at the end of things, sick and scared and dying, and know that by all human computation their load of sin is too great to expect mercy, and it is too late even to pray! Every pastor and chaplain has such experiences—then reaches for this text! God bless thee, Good Thief on the Cross! Thou hast been an evangelist, a preacher of the Gospel, lo, these two thousand years, and will continue to be until thy Lord cometh in His glory!

Crisp and definite and final was the assurance of the Savior: *"Today, in Paradise."* There is to be no waiting period, no struggle through purgatory, and no depending on the incidental petitions of friends and relatives, or the hired prayers of professionals. What a bulwark of assurance against those who would have us believe otherwise, or against our own hearts, or the Evil One!

> There is a fountain filled with blood
> Drawn from Immanuel's veins,
> And sinners plunged beneath that flood
> Lose all their guilty stains.
>
> The dying thief rejoiced to see
> That fountain in his day;
> And there have I, as vile as he,
> Washed all my sins away.
>
> Dear dying Lamb, Thy precious blood
> Shall never lose its power,
> Till all the ransomed Church of God
> Be saved, to sin no more.
>
> WILLIAM COWPER, 1731-1800

PRAYER

Jesus, pitying the sighs of the thief who near Thee dies,
Promising him Paradise: Hear us, Holy Jesus!
May we in our guilt and shame, still Thy love and mercy claim,
Calling humbly on Thy name: Hear us, Holy Jesus!
May our hearts to Thee incline, looking from our cross to Thine;
Cheer our souls with hope divine: Hear us, Holy Jesus!

From the Litany for Good Friday

113

Woman, behold your son

THE SEVEN LAST WORDS · THIRD WORD

When Jesus saw his mother, and the disciple whom he loved standing near, he said to his mother, "Woman, behold your son!" Then he said to the disciple, "Behold your mother!" And from that hour the disciple took her to his own home.
John 19:26

JESUS' foster father, Joseph, seems to have been dead by now. Matthew states (13:35) that our Lord had four brothers, James, Joses, Simon, and Jude, and that He also had sisters; they may have been by a former marriage of Joseph. John says (7:5) that His family did not believe in Him as the Messiah until after the resurrection. But His mother did. John was Jesus' cousin ("kinsman"). He was the youngest, most tenderhearted and understanding of the disciples, and had a special place among them all as "John the Beloved." John and Mary therefore had a unique place over against each other. As for Mary, the mother of our Lord according to His

114

earthly nature, there is no need, and no Scriptural authority whatsoever, for building her up in the fantastic, grotesque manner that has been done by certain Churches, making out of her a divinity and the Queen of Heaven, with impossible prerogatives. The Gospels mention her with respect, but only occasionally, and after Acts 1:14 she is not mentioned at all. Let us honor her for what the Word of God says that she was, the mother of the Savior and the one who understood Him best. Let us honor her for her humility and quiet ways, her trust, faith, and obedience, her patience, sweet graciousness, and winsome goodness, and her faithful service to Him who was also her Lord and Savior. That is enough distinction and divinity for any daughter of Eve!

In honoring Mary of Nazareth, we honor all good women. Family life and the stability of the home, which are the bulwark of any nation and civilization worthy of survival, are the unique responsibility of womankind primarily. The men can go wrong, they can be brutes and beasts. But if their women are strong and decent and true, the race is saved and the next generation can start over again! It is not for nothing that the aphorism has grown up: "Behind every good and great man is a good woman!" And the hand that rocks the cradle does rule the world! These observations we make, gentle maid of Nazareth, Mater Dolorosa, Mother of Sorrows, as we stand with thee beneath the cross and try to fathom and share thy sorrow and the sharp stab of the prophecy made long years before when the

115

Crucified One was an infant in thy arms and old Simeon's blessing faded into the prophecy:

Behold, this child is set for the fall and rising of many in
    Israel,
And for a sign that is spoken against
(and a sword will pierce through your own soul also),
That thoughts out of many hearts may be revealed.

(Luke 2:34)

PRAYER-HYMN

Near the cross was Mary weeping,
There her mournful station keeping,
Gazing on her dying Son.
There, with speechless grief oppressed,
Anguish-stricken and distressed;
Through her soul the sword had gone.

Who upon that Sufferer gazing,
Bowed in sorrow so amazing,
Would not with His mother mourn?
'Twas our sins brought Him from heaven,
These the cruel nails had driven;
All His griefs for us were borne.

When no eye its pity gave us,
When there was no arm to save us,
He His love and power displayed;
By His stripes He wrought our healing,
By His death our life revealing,
He for us the ransom paid.

Jesus, may Thy love constrain us,
That from sin we may refrain us,
In Thy griefs may deeply grieve.
Thee our best affections giving,
To Thy glory ever living,
May we in Thy glory live!

Famous medieval song of sorrow, "Stabat Mater Dolorosa," ascribed by many to Jacoponus da Todi (d. ca. 1306). Translation by H. Mills, 1845.

116

Why hast Thou forsaken me?

THE SEVEN LAST WORDS · FOURTH WORD

My God, my God, why hast thou forsaken me?
Matthew 27:46

IT WAS about noon, and now terrible things began to happen. The earth became dark with an unearthly darkness. Terror was in the air. Awed and fearful, friends and foes alike began to realize that this was indeed no ordinary crucifixion. From noon-day until mid-afternoon, the darkness lasted. Then, all of a sudden, in the ghastly gloom a cry was heard. It came from the Figure on the central cross: *"Eli! Eli! Lama sa-bach-thani!"* "My God! My God! Why hast thou forsaken me?" These are the most terrible words in the Bible; they are the cry of the damned.

The agony of Gethsemane was upon Him again, only this time it was even worse. There was now no connecting link, no union with the Father, to bear Him up, and no angel to strengthen Him! It is impossible for mortals to fully realize the depths of despair in that cry, because we have no experience whereby to measure it. Separation from God is the punishment of the lost—not the self-imposed, pride-nurtured, imaginary separation that the atheist and smart-aleck himself erects, but the final Ultimate, the Real Thing, as when God almighty Himself decrees it!

As long as our Lord was conscious of the backing and presence of His heavenly Father He could go on in strength and confidence, and in full possession of His divinity. But it was a part of the mystery of the atonement that also these were to be taken away from Him for a season, and that He had to experience the despair of the lost. Again His cry was in the words of the twenty-second Psalm and in the language of His childhood. Even in the delirium of this terrible climax to His suffering His mind reached out for His psalm book, and in its language did He speak.

The cry came without warning, and none of the multitude were prepared for it. Furthermore, many of them were not close enough to make it out clearly; and others did not understand the language that He used. "Eli! Eli!"—He is calling for Elias (Elijah), they said. Elijah was the greatest of the so-called oral prophets of the Old Testament. He is the last prophet named there (Malachi 4:5); and John the Baptist, as the forerunner of the Messiah, was given his name by simile. Elijah was also a part of the great vision on the Mount of Transfiguration, with Christ and Moses. So there was more of fear than of derision when some of the spectators said to one another, "Let us wait and see if Elijah will come and save him." They waited, awed and uneasy.

And yet this prayer also, which was not really a prayer but a cry of "Why?" was answered. This is a comfort to us who pray so much in the language of a cry. In moments of extremity and despair in our own little lives, when our prayers are only an inarticulate cry of anguish, like a child's sob in the night, it is good to know that the answer will come at last. For no one has ever cried to Him in vain.

PRAYER

Jesus, whelmed by fears unknown, with our evil left alone, while no light from heaven is shown: hear us, holy Jesus.

When we seem in vain to pray, and our hope seems far away, in the darkness be our stay: hear us, holy Jesus.

Though no Father seems to hear, though no light our spirits cheer, may we know that God is near! Hear us, holy Jesus. Amen.

Litany for Good Friday, Fourth Word.

I thirst

THE SEVEN LAST WORDS · FIFTH WORD

*After this Jesus, knowing that all was now finished, said
(to fulfill the scripture), "I thirst."*   John 19:28

IF THE cry in the Fourth Word was that of Jesus'
soul, then that in the Fifth may be said to have
been that of His body. It is also reminiscent of more
than one occasion in His ministry when He spoke
of water and of thirst: At the well in Samaria when
He said to the woman, "Whoever drinks of the water
that I shall give him will never thirst," and she replied, "Sir, give me this water!" And when He said:
"Whoever gives to one of these little ones even a
cup of cold water, shall not lose his reward." And
in the Judgment Scene: "I was hungry and you gave
me food; thirsty and you gave me drink." Now He
who had poured out so many a cup of blessing was
Himself in need of that cup—He who was the Water

and Fountain of Life! This moment was the closest that our Lord ever came to asking a favor of His enemies. And yet when He received it He turned it aside.

"I thirst!" The soldiers were more considerate than His countrymen, for they did something about it. The Gospels are not clear as to the details of their procedure, and the commentaries have struggled with the texts to harmonize them. Perhaps the simplest and most practical explanation comes the closest: One of the soldiers, kinder than his companions, ran to his jug or bottle containing the cheap, strong, sour wine which was all that a soldier could afford, removed the sponge or sop which acted as a sort of stopper, soaked it well, and put it up to Jesus' mouth on the end of his spear. Or perhaps he pulled up a nearby plant called "hyssop," which was aromatic and thought to be medicinal, and fixed the sop on that. His rough remark as he did so (cf. Luke 23:36-37) may have been to cover up in the presence of his companions, the weakness of showing kindness!

But Jesus would not accept it. He wanted neither stimulant nor sedative, but would drink His cup of woe to the dregs, in full consciousness and without help. He may also have been quoting once more from His hymnbook (Psalm 69:21), whose contents kept running through His mind all that terrible Good Friday, especially those texts having to do with the suffering Messiah Servant. For our Lord was fulfilling Scripture that day!

There is another kind of thirst, the kind that Jesus referred to in the opening beatitudes of His Sermon on the Mount: "Blessed are those who hunger and thirst for righteousness, for they shall be satisfied." It is not inconsistent with our text if we pause before the Christ and His Fifth Word from the cross and check ourselves in the matter of those cups of water and other acts of kindness that He has enjoined upon us, and also how deep and genuine is our thirst after the Kingdom of God and His righteousness. He who said, "I thirst!" because of His body needs and sufferings and to fulfill Scripture, but who laid them aside, both in the day of His temptation in the wilderness and again on the cross, bids us have higher hungerings and thirstings than those of this body and life!

PRAYER

Jesus, in Thy thirst and pain, while Thy wounds Thy life-blood drain, thirsting more our love to gain: hear us, holy Jesus!

Thirst for us in mercy still; all Thy holy work fulfill; satisfy Thy loving will: hear us, holy Jesus!

May we thirst Thy love to know; lead us, in our sin and woe, where the healing waters flow: hear us, holy Jesus! Amen.

Litany for Good Friday, Fifth Word.

Into Thy hands

THE SEVEN LAST WORDS · SEVENTH WORD*

Father, into thy hands I commit my spirit! Luke 23:46

SINCE the beginning of time philosophers and
religionists have been busy telling men how
to live. And not a few of them, even of those with
humanistic and pagan backgrounds, have come up
with good and brave and beautiful aphorisms and
formulas—others, of course, with horrible ones! But
how many of them have had the wits or vision to
tell us how to die or to speak with conviction
about the Great Beyond? Homer was unable to,
as were the classic Greek thinkers after him, and
the philosophers since their time. Socrates doubtless
came the closest, with a vague but beautiful trust.

---

*To fit the pattern of this book, we have placed the seventh Word ahead
of the Sixth, so that we might use the theme "It is finished" as the climax
of the series, in the sermon for the last Sunday in Lent. The two "Words"
may be part of the same utterance.

All of them have asked the questions over and over —but with no assurance of an answer! Whether we put it in the simple vagary of kindly Jessie Pounds:

> Beautiful Isle of Somewhere!
> Land of the true, where we live anew,
> Beautiful Isle of Somewhere.

or we say with Arthur Clough:

> Where lies the land, to which the ship would go?
> Far, far ahead, is all her seamen know,

the answer is just as uncertain and unsatisfactory. Without help we can only yearn and wonder. Only by revelation and faith can the answer come clearly. And we have it in Christ.

Various indeed have been the manner and advice of men on how to die. "Let us eat, drink, and be merry, for tomorrow we die!" says the epicure. "Live beyond good and evil; master mind and master race are what count," said Nietzsche. "Life is a blind, impelling force, and pain and unsatisfied wants are its portion to the end, which is death," said Schopenhauer. And defiant Sara Teasdale writes:

> I would not have a god come in
> To shield me suddenly from sin,
> And set my house of life to rights . . .
> Rather my own frail guttering lights . . .
> Rather the terror of the nights . . .
> Rather be lost than let my soul
> Slip vaguely from my own control!
> Of my own spirit, let me be
> In sole though feeble mastery!

124

What an end! May God have mercy on such folks and their wild defiance.

The Son of God was content and happy to say: "Father, into thy hands I commit my spirit," and then bow His head and breathe His last. In Him we, too, can die calmly and confidently and fear our graves as little as we do our beds. Finally we note that they did not kill the Lord of Life! He *gave* His life, and He took it again on Easter morning! Neither soldiers nor demons could force His life from Him.

We who are pastors still close the eyes of the dying and quote the words of the Saviour: "Father, into Thy hands we commend his spirit, her spirit." And when comes our own turn to leave this world, may there be those at hand who love us, to help us through with the same words, and close our tired eyes with faith in the same Savior, who said the words first!

PRAYER

Jesus, all Thy labor vast, all Thy woe and conflict past; yielding up Thy soul at last: hear us, holy Jesus!

When the death-shades round us lower, guard us from the tempter's power, keep us in that trial hour: hear us, holy Jesus!

May Thy life and death supply grace to live and grace to die, grace to reach the home on high: hear us, holy Jesus.

Litany for Good Friday, Seventh Word.

It is finished

THE SEVEN LAST WORDS · SIXTH WORD

It is finished. John 19:30

IN THE Garden Jesus had prayed: "My Father, if it be possible, let this cup pass from me; nevertheless, not as I will, but as Thou wilt." Now on the cross, with that terrible cry of His soul: "My God, my God, why hast thou forsaken me!" and with the cry of His body: "I thirst," the cup was drained, drained to its last bitter dregs. "It is finished!"—it was with a loud voice that He uttered these words. Many of the multitude again doubtless heard them only as another cry (cf. Mark 15:36), many still do. How little they understand!

"It is finished!" It was a cry of victory, of triumph! All His life on earth, all His long story of service and suffering and sacrifice had focused on this battle and this moment. And now, like one who has fought his way through a dreadful sickness, the long build-up of its fever, and through to the final climax —will he make it or must he perish?—the sweat, the struggle, the delirium, the labored breathing, the anxious waiting! And then, like the sun from behind the clouds—the crisis is passed and the patient emerges on the other side; consciousness has returned, the fever is gone, the eyes are clear, the temperature is down, and the pulse is normal and steady!

"It is finished!" It was a cry of liberation. The job is done, the war is over—we are free! In the land of music, how tremendously Edvard Grieg sang of this in his own failing health, the year before he died, using a folk-song of his people and Brorson's text:

> *Guds søn har gjort mig fri*
> *fra Satans tyranni!*
>
> God's Son has set me free
> From Satan's tyranny! . . .
> Yes, free, yes, free! Free! Free! Free!
> God's Son has set me free!

"It is finished!" It was the cry of completion, of finality. One question that pastors and chaplains hear perhaps more frequently than any other, not only from the young, but from gray-haired veterans of the faith, is: "How can I be sure that I am saved? Read me the passages again! Some tell me that this is not enough." And we open the old Book and read: "It is finished!"

"Though your sins are like scarlet,
    they shall be as white as snow;
Though they are red like crimson,
    they shall become like wool."

Isaiah 1:18

"Come to me, all who labor and are heavy-laden,
    and I will give you rest."

Matthew 11:28

"Do not fear; only believe." Luke 8:50.

"God shows his love for us in that while we were yet sinners
    Christ died for us! . . .
We also rejoice in God through our Lord Jesus Christ,
    Through whom we have now received our reconciliation."

Romans 5:8,"

(Indeed that whole fifth chapter of Romans echoes to
the finality and assurance of "It is finished!")

But there are also other notes to this mighty
chorus! Some day the Almighty will say for the last
time to the wicked of this world—the dictators, the
belligerent godless, the rampant antichrists and evil-
doers that plague each generation and make hide-
ous and unhappy the lives and times of the decent
and peace loving—"It is finished, you are through—
now get out of here, with your ambitions, your ideologies, and your carryings-on!" And the cry of the
oppressed, the poor, the bereaved, and the brutal-
ized, in whom Christ is crucified anew: "How long,
O Lord, how long," will be answered at last. And
for all the sleepless who toss about and wait for

128

morn, the sin-sick, those who suffer from physical and mental maladies, the world's miserable, struggling with oft recurring pains, fears, worries, situations, the futility of life, and the dogging of the Evil One—for them also there will be the answer and the comfort of God: "This too will have an end and there will be peace at last" through Him who said, "It is finished!" Everything has an end. For the pomp of kings and the glorification of fools, the antics of megalomaniacs, and all the inequalities, injustices, and maladjustments of this world—some day there will come word from on high: "*Consummatum est!*" "It is finished!" And for the lives of little you and me, and the little arc of our times, and for the wide world itself, the epitaph will be written: "It is finished."

And *then*, like inter-spacial travelers who have fought free of the gravity and atmosphere and pull of this planet and been released to the timeless, spaceless eternity of the stars, we shall be free and a part of Him in His final heaven for ever and ever, Him who said, "It is finished!"

THE STARRY NIGHT

We are such little men when the stars come out,
So small under the open maw of the night,
That we must shout and pound the table and drive wild,
And gather dollars and madly dance and drink deep,
And send the great Birds flying to drop death!
When the stars come out we are such little men
That we must arm ourselves in glare and thunder,
Or cave in on our own dry littleness.

129

We are such little men when the stars come out!
Ah, God behind the stars, touch with your finger
This mite of meaningless dust, and give it substance.
I am so little under the frown of the night!
Be You my body, You my eyes, my lips,
My hands, my feet, my heart-beat, and my hunger,
That I may face the infinite spaces and live;
And stand in quietness, when the stars come out!

HERMANN HAGEDORN, 1882

PRAYER

*Jesus, all our ransom paid, all Thy Father's will obeyed,
by Thy sufferings perfect made: hear us, holy Jesus!*

*Save us in our soul's distress, be our help to cheer and
bless, while we grow in holiness: hear us, holy Jesus!*

*Brighten all our heavenward way with an ever holier ray,
till we pass to perfect day: hear us, holy Jesus! Amen.*

Litany for Good Friday, Sixth Word.

The quick and the dead testify

And behold, the curtain of the temple was torn in two, from top to bottom; and the earth shook. . . . When the centurion and those who were with him, keeping watch over Jesus, saw the earthquake . . . they were filled with awe, and said, "Truly this was a son of God."　　　Matthew 27:51ff.

THE tragedy of the ages was over. It was three o'clock in the afternoon of Friday, April seven, 30 A.D., according to the best computations. Then came the earthquake. With that peculiar subterranean rumble that is so often a characteristic, it built up into its awful convulsions. The three crosses swayed in the unnatural twilight, and the whole landscape trembled and shook. The huge temple rocked on its massive foundations, and the great curtain that separated the Holy of Holies from the Holy Place, was rent in twain from top to bottom. Ere the day was over, reports began to come in of apochryphal events accompanying the earthquake, of graves opened and visions of the dead arising and appearing among the people. The quick and the dead, and nature itself, were bearing witness to the passing of their Lord. Terror-stricken, the crowd on Calvary Hill huddled together, or rushed from the scene, beating their breast. Awed, the centurion in charge of the executions exclaimed: "Truly this was a righteous man, this was the Son of God."

The soldiers recovered first—their training and their harsh military experiences would account for that. Furthermore, they were under orders: to get the crucifixions over with, the bodies out of the way, and the whole mess cleaned up by nightfall. For the Jewish Sabbath was coming on. It began when the sun went down on Friday, and it was already late in the afternoon. The Jewish leaders were not troubled about crucifixions and the death of the innocent, but they were squeamish about their Sabbath. The people recovered also, as they always do, no matter with what voice God or nature speaks. The events of the day were doubtless comfortably and satisfactorily explained: earthquakes were a natural phenomenon; they had had them before and would doubtless have them again, and furthermore there were no casualties to speak of. As for the reports concerning the dead, they could be laid to the fears and superstitions of the people. Gradually the Good Friday darkness also lifted, the sun shone again, and nature settled down. But for those directly concerned and whose eyes had been opened, Good Friday's events were not forgotten so easily—they were indelible and nothing would ever be the same again, never, never, never. But even for many of them it would take time before a full realization of the tremendousness of what had happened would be granted them. One thing, however, was freely admitted by everyone: the likes of that Figure in the center would never be seen again. He was a righteous man and a hero! "Truly he was a Son of God!"

But now He was dead. What's great about being dead? Is not, after all, a live coward better than a dead hero? A living mouse than a dead lion? The scoundrel that survives than the martyr that expires? Ask Judas! Ask Pilate! Ask Caiaphas!

A BALLAD OF WONDER

My Lord came to me once a King; a crown was in His hair.
I never knew that anything could be so regal fair.
My Lord came to me once a King. I stopped my dream to stare.

My Lord came once—(Shall it be said I did but dream He came?)—
A crown of thorns was on His head, but in His heart a flame.
He came alone, unheralded, and signed me with His name.
I Am No More the Same. ELEANOR SLATER

DEDICATION

I told Jesus it would be alright
If He changed my name, changed my name.
I told Jesus it would be alright
If He changed my name.

133

Jesus told me I'd have to live humble
If He changed my name, changed my name.
Jesus told me I'd have to live humble
If He changed my name.

Jesus told me that the world would hate me
If He changed my name, changed my name.
Jesus told me that the world would hate me
If He changed my name.

I told Jesus it would be alright
If He changed my name, changed my name.
I told Jesus it would be alright
If He changed my name.

Negro spiritual, as sung by
MARIAN ANDERSON

That scripture might be fulfilled

So the soldiers came and broke the legs of the first, and of the other who had been crucified with him; but when they came to Jesus and saw that he was already dead, they did not break his legs. But one of the soldiers pierced his side with a spear. . . . These things took place that the scripture might be fulfilled. John 19:32ff.

SO THAT the crucified might not linger on too long and their bodies remain over the Sabbath, orders were issued to dispatch them at once. It was done quickly and easy-like, with clubs! From one cross to the next the soldiers went. A crash-crack of splintered bones, a dying moan or two, and it was over. But when they got to the central cross, the man with the club paused. This was That Other

135

One! The soldier raised his club—and paused again. Why? True, the man was already dead, but why should that save Him a clubbing? The soldier lowered his club. Perhaps he never knew why to his dying day, except that this was That Other One! And yet he had orders. He reached for his spear, instead, and plunged it into Jesus' side. And there came forth blood and water. This illiterate heathen soldier was fulfilling Scripture that day!

The Scripture passages were two. The first one was: "Not a bone of him shall be broken" (Exodus 12:46; Numbers 9:12; Psalm 34:20). The second was: "They shall look on him whom they have pierced" (Zechariah 12:10), *i.e.*, not him whose bones they had broken. It all went back to that first Passover in Moses' day (Exodus 12). Jesus was its Messianic fulfillment. At the last Passover sacrifice, "the Lamb of God that taketh away the sin of the world," Jesus' body had to be respected, by the very token of Moses and the first Passover lamb. His sacrificial blood could be spilled, but His body could not be crushed.

To a Christian it is curious and helpful to note how this illiterate pagan had a role in God's plan that day. For it may be an indication that we, too, who are His very own children, are not unused either, but have a part in God's purposes, however, small! The writer of these pages is certain that some day it will be given to us to know this and rejoice in it.

History is full of examples of those who have served God unwittingly or with no realization of their value. The mothers of great and good men are often such. Nancy Hanks brought forth her little son and called him Abraham, Abraham Lincoln. The patriots who fought and died at Lexington and Concord doubtless thought that they were only defending hedges and homes against an invader. How could they know that they were bloody midwives bringing to birth a mighty nation? The soldiers that fired and fled or fired and died at the Battle of Bull Run —how could they know that they were important in the saving of that nation? In the religious and spiritual world, too, it happens over and over again. A peddler hands Richard Baxter a pamphlet. He reads it and becomes a Christian. He in turn does some writing and converts Phillip Dodderidge, who in turn writes among other things hymns and blesses thousands. One of these is William Wilberforce; and after him it goes on to his son, and from him to William Pitt, and through them both to Gladstone. Who started this chain reaction of goodness? An unknown peddler a full century before! Thus God works. With God nothing is wasted, neither with things nor with men. We are doubtless, all of us, fulfilling Bible passages all our lives long and carrying out the purposes of our Lord. It is good to know this. Let us pray God that we may not spoil it, but that He will make use of us and give us the privilege and fun of knowing that in our little way, by His grace, we are helpers and partners with His holy Son!

We go back to the man with the spear:

137

PRAYER

Rock of Ages, cleft for me: let me hide myself in Thee! Let the water and the blood, from Thy riven side which flowed, be of sin the double cure; save me from its guilt and power.

While I draw this fleeting breath, when mine eyelids close in death, when I soar to worlds unknown, see Thee on Thy judgment throne—Rock of Ages, cleft for me: Let me hide myself in Thee!

AUGUSTUS M. TOPLADY, 1776

Post-mortem friends

After this Joseph of Arimathea . . . asked Pilate that he might take away the body of Jesus; and Pilate gave him leave . . . Nicodemus also, . . . came, bringing a mixture of myrrh and aloes, about a hundred pounds' weight.

John 19:38f.

A BOUT this time friends began to appear. Those who had not had the courage to espouse Him while alive were now very brave and busy honoring Him after He was dead. Let us not judge them too harshly. It is easier (and safer) to acclaim a man after he is dead than to praise him against the crowd while he is yet alive.

There were two men whose names stand out with something like honor in connection with the trial and crucifixion of our Lord. They both seem to have been members of the Sanhedrin, but they did not consent to His death. The first one was Joseph of Arimathea. The Gospels record that he was a disciple of Jesus—but secretly for fear of the Jews; and that he was a good and righteous man, "looking for the Kingdom of God." Also that he was wealthy and that he offered his own newly hewn-out tomb as the resting place for the murdered Nazarene. The second post mortem friend was Nicodemus. We remember him as the one who came to Jesus at night and sat with Him under the stars discussing discipleship and the new Birth (John 3). He had gone away, still slow of heart to believe and accept, but with an intense admiration for the Teacher, and in his uncertain, groping way, His disciple. Together, he and Joseph of Arimathea had Jesus taken down from the cross with tenderness and respect, washed, anointed, wrapped in linen, and laid away with decency and decorum. They had to work fast, for the twilight of the Sabbath was already upon them.

There is no mention of what became of the two wretches that were crucified with Jesus. Their bodies were doubtless thrown into a common pit and shoveled under, according to the time-honored custom with those who have neither friend nor relative willing to own them. We doubt if Jesus would have permitted that, if He had remained alive—not even for the one who reviled Him. To point the lesson—there is something cruel and pathetic about a pauper's burial, even in communities where the county commissioners are so generous as to foot the bill for coffin, shroud, and grave. Any pastor who has walked with the undertaker ahead of a simple black casket,

140

without a single flower, mourner, or tear; or any layman who has left work and donated his services to help carry the corpse and lend a hand with the ropes that lowered the friendless one into his rough-box, will appreciate the pathos and loneliness of such a scene. This writer has himself halted at the graveside at such a moment, long enough to pluck a simple wildflower and lay on the bleak casket, in the mute testimony of a blossom that God is love and pities everybody!

Well, since our Savior was content to yield His body to a borrowed grave, it doubtless matters little where and how these poor bodies of ours are disposed of when we are through with this world. Embalming fluid, the make-up of the dead, bronze and rosewood and ebony caskets, choirs, eulogies, ceremonials, serried ranks and banks of hot-house flowers, massive granite, and "everlasting care," mean very, very little in the appraisal of the Almighty.

A GRAVESIDE HYMN

Here all life's pathways blending, we reach the grave's steep side, life's pomp and glory ending, its pleasures and its pride! Here man's ambition waneth, so restless from his birth; its final goal attaineth—the bosom of the earth!

But He whose love us follows, from cradle to the grave, and all life's journey hallows, with mighty power to save, forbids us now to sorrow, as those of hope forlorn; but points to God's tomorrow, the resurrection morn.

N. F. S. GRUNDTVIG, 1783-1872:
"Her mødes alle veie" (Tr. L. N. F., 1948)

Perhaps no hymn of Grundtvig's has been so much used at gravesides as this.

The women

There were also many women there, . . . who had followed Jesus from Galilee, ministering to him. . . . And Joseph took the body, . . . and laid it in his own new tomb, which he had hewn in the rock. . . . Mary Magdalene and the other Mary were there, sitting opposite the tomb. Matthew 27:55ff.

THE most compassionate of all who followed Jesus to His doom were the women. There was a considerable group of them. They had banded together back in the early days of Jesus' ministry to look after His simple daily wants and those of His disciples. Luke (chapter 8) describes them as a sort of ladies aid serving the Lord and His Twelve. Among these women there were several who by an interesting coincidence bore the same name; there was Mary the mother of our Lord, Mary the mother of two of the apostles, Mary the wife of Cleopas, and Mary Magdalene, out of whom we are told that the Lord drove seven demons. They followed the procession to Calvary as closely as they could, weeping in helpless pity. Now, as soon as the crucifixion was over, they were on hand again to render service. When the soldiers had withdrawn with their clubs and spears, and the men with ladders and ropes were through, the women took up their task. Tenderly they removed the cruel crown of thorns, washed His bruised body, cleansed His gaping wounds, and composed His sacred limbs for their last resting place, as they thought. Then they helped wrap Him in clean grave-linen, with fragrant decay-resisting herbs and spices about Him, weeping and exclaiming as they worked. But there was not enough time to finish because nightfall had already arrived. So they noted carefully where His tomb was, watched as the heavy stone was rolled into place before the entrance, and saw the guard set up its sentry. Then they departed sorrowfully, determined to come back just as soon as the Sabbath was over to complete their task. They who were last at the sealed sepulchre were also to be the first at the open tomb!

These faithful women, who watched over Jesus in life and wept over Him in death, are emblematic of good women of every age and place in the Church. In our day they and their devotion are the example and challenge of every ladies aid, parish auxiliary, and sisterhood in the land. There have been more than many times, as many a pastor can testify, when they have been the first at the cradle and the last at the grave.

The Lord whom these pious women had served was now dead and laid away. Even though He had spoken clearly and insistently of a resurrection, they dared not follow through on His prediction and be literal about it. Not until they were initiated into the glory of Easter would they dare do that. But they believed on Him, and they trusted in Him, somehow, somehow! It is impossible to believe that the women went home that night without some sense of hope, some instinctive feeling that this was not all, and that something does happen after death. But they didn't know when, and they didn't know how! It would have to wait until the great Tomorrow!

Let us not believe in death! Let us believe in life —life everlasting in Christ Jesus!

END OF A JOURNEY

I have seen death too often to believe in death.
It is not an ending, but a withdrawal—
As one who finishes a long journey,
Stills the motor,
Turns off the lights,
Steps from his car,
And walks up the path
To the home that awaits him.

DON BLANDING

PRAYER

Dear Lord: Keep my faith strong and steady! Give me opportunities to serve, and teach me the joy of that service, so that when I am gone I may be remembered, not for what I have accumulated for others to quarrel over, or the bones

I have crushed, or the spears I have brandished, or the weapons I have forged, or the castles and fortresses I have reared, or the destruction I have wrought, or the fears I have engendered, or the times I have forced my will through! But by Thy grace let me be remembered for some little good that I have done, for the times I have been faithful, for the little oases of flowers and fruit and shade I planted and left behind me where I walked and tarried. Grant that there may be at least a few memories by those whom I loved and whose love I enjoyed, and a kindly sigh or two: "We wish that he could have stayed a little longer—there was something wholesome and good about him; he meant well and he tried; and we felt helped and ennobled when he had been around!" Dear Lord, by Thy grace and Thy love, let me so live and so die! Amen.

Make it as secure as you can

Next day . . . the chief priests and the Pharisees gathered before Pilate and said, "Sir, we remember how that impostor said while he was still alive, 'After three days I will rise again.' Therefore order the sepulchre to be made secure until the third day, lest his disciples go and steal him away, and tell the people, 'He is arisen from the dead,' and the last fraud will be worse than the first." Pilate said, "You have a guard of soldiers; go, make it as secure as you can." So they went, and made the sepulchre secure by sealing the stone and setting a guard. Matthew 27:62ff.

THE enemies of Jesus were not through yet; they would not quit until every last one of the Twelve was dead, plus Stephen and Paul and Barnabas and a host of others. After Herod and Pilate and Caiaphas, there would be Nero and Caligula; and on down the ages there would be an antichrist or more for every generation, somewhere, to crucify Christ anew, to bury Him deep, deep, and

146

to plague His followers. Jesus' enemies remembered His words about resurrection better than His friends did. Back of their sneers and precautions lay a fear: "What, after all, if it should go as He had said?" Pilate had given them a military guard and said, "Make it as secure as you can!" They did.

All to whom it was given to know that Jesus arose from the dead, by actual sight of Him, by hearing His voice, and even by touching Him—and they were many, since Paul records (I Corinthians 15:6) that He was seen by more than five hundred at one time—all of these and all who have witnessed or had a part in the very lively history of His Church ever since, can afford a little smile at the frantic efforts of the scribes and Pharisees and their soldiers! For all they did was in vain.

APOSTROPHE TO THE GUARDS. Set your sentries and post your guards! Pilate and the temple leaders ordered it, you know! Present arms—your clubs, your spears, and your swords! Salute, click your heels, and pace back and forth—you've got Him in there, haven't you, stiff and dead? But maybe He'll come out and fight you anyway. His followers fled at the very beginning, but you never know, they may return and overpower you. Better post the other side of the area too; this sepulchre is hewn out of rock, but they might dig through and get Him out nevertheless. You can't be too careful! There have been body-snatchers before your time and there will be after you, too. Abraham Lincoln's body was almost stolen, also, from its mausoleum—if you could have

147

lived long enough to hear about it! Pay no attention to lightning, earthquakes, or angels—you have the backing of the Big Wheels of this earth: Pilate, Herod, the temple leaders of a nation, and Beelzebub himself! Poor simpletons, to try to thwart the rising Christ! But keep it up, Boys! Keep on trying! You are not alone, then or since. Then, afterward, to hide your failure and save your face, lie about it and tell those who hired you that He is there yet, or that somebody did steal Him after all. You know that Easter is day after tomorrow, don't you; and that after that He will be coming and going among us for forty days? Why don't you grab Him then, and hustle Him back into His tomb and order Him to stay there? From then on He is going to be with us forever, even unto the end of the world. Couldn't you do something about that too? So keep it up, ha! ha! Watch that tomb! Keep trying! And phooey to you! We will sit here opposite the sepulchre, with the women who watched, and wait it out!

> I will repudiate the lie
> Men tell of life;
> How it will pass
> As fragile flower, or butterfly,
> Whose dust shall nourish
> April grass.
>
> Since One, for love, died on a tree
> And in the stony
> Tomb has lain,
> Behold I show a mystery:
> All sepulchres
> Are sealed in vain!
>
> JOHN RICHARD MORELAND

148

This is not the end

Now I would remind you, brethren, in what terms I preached to you the gospel, which you received, in which you stand, by which you are saved, if you hold it fast. . . . For I delivered to you as of first importance what I also received, that Christ died for our sins in accordance with the scriptures, that he was buried, that he was raised on the third day in accordance with the scriptures. . . . Whether then it was I or they [i.e., the other Apostles], *so we preach and so you believed. . . . If Christ has not been raised, your faith is futile and you are still in your sins. Then those also who have fallen asleep in Christ have perished. If in this life we who are in Christ have only hope, we are of all men most to be pitied. But in fact Christ has been raised from the dead, the first fruits of those who have fallen asleep. For as by a man came death, by a man has come also the resurrection of the dead. For as in Adam all die, so also in Christ shall all be made alive.* I Corinthians 15:1ff.

SLOWLY the Jewish Sabbath wore itself to a close. It is not known for certain what the disciples did that day. We can only conjecture. Most likely they went back to that sacred Upper Room

149

that had already become their shrine and rallying place. Heartbroken by all that had taken place, ashamed of their own craven part in the tragedy, fearful of what the enemy might do next, and with vivid memories of the convulsions of nature when He died, they hardly knew where to turn or what to expect. Over it all hung the great sorrow over His death. Doubtless, during those heavy hours of the Sabbath, they were trying to pull themselves together and get used to the new emptiness in their lives. To be sure, He had told them that what had happened was going to happen, and that He would rise again and be with them, and had even directed them to go back to Galilee and await Him there. But that was too good to be true. It was impossible, and they dismissed it from their minds. It was simply His way of speaking, His way of using similes. No, it was in their memories that He would be with them; it was with the charm of His ways and the impress of His teachings that He would continue to inspire and lead them. Truly, they would not forget that either—but farther than that their minds refused to go—all the Gospels bear witness to this. It was no wishful thinking on the part of the disciples, therefore, that created an Easter myth. They were as hard to convince of its actuality as the most skeptical of their enemies (cf. John 20:25)—so much so that one almost wonders at it, in view of all that He had said and His own miracles of raising the dead. They were convinced against their will.

We, too, pause in awe and wonder before the

sublimity of Easter. It is either the most stupendous fact in human existence, or else it was nothing. If the resurrection of Jesus Christ is true, then all that follows with it is also true. Then, under His divine power, the souls of men have leaped out of the limitations of animal existence and the finite, past and beyond the terminals of birth and death, of time and space, and achieved heaven and immortality. It is the final act of reconciliation and of glory, between the Creator and His highest creature. Any meaner conception of Deity would be worth nothing—anything short of victory over sin and death, anything less than immortality with God and in the company of other immortals, would be but inadequate divinity. God had to do all this, or be untrue to Himself!

Yes, we stand in awe before the glory of Easter. But our gracious heavenly Father has given us the means to grasp and appropriate it and enjoy it. It is *faith* that dares to make the leap and accept it and to live and die by it. This, then, is the goal and terminal point of "A Journey to Easter." *Soli Deo Gloria!*

PRAYER HYMN

My faith looks up to Thee, Thou Lamb of Calvary, Saviour divine!
Now hear me while I pray, take all my guilt away, O let me from this day, be wholly Thine.

May Thy rich grace impart strength to my fainting heart, my zeal inspire.

151

As Thou hast died for me, O may my love to Thee pure, warm, and changeless be, a living fire!
While life's dark maze I tread, and griefs around me spread, be Thou my Guide!
Bid darkness turn to day, wipe sorrow's tears away, nor let me ever stray from Thee aside.

When ends life's transient dream, when death's cold, sullen stream shall o'er me roll,
Blest Saviour, then, in love, fear and distress remove; O bear me safe above, a ransomed soul. Amen.

RAY PALMER, 1830